The

Stream

of

Time

LEN HARRIS

Lovstad Publishing
Poynette, Wisconsin
Lovstadpublishing@live.com

ISBN: 0615762247
ISBN-13: 978-0615762241

Printed in the United States of America

Cover photo by Len Harris

Cover design by Lovstad Publishing

I would like to dedicate this book to the women in my life.

My Mother, Jane, who gave me the "The Gift"
that will help me throughout my life.

To my beautiful daughter, Anna, who never
lets me forget to listen for "The Wind In The Trees."

And to my wife, Barb, who loves me unconditionally,
gave me the inspiration to write this book, and who
never complains about my "Muddy Boots."

Contents

The

Stream

of

Time

LEN HARRIS

ONCE IN A LIFETIME

I really need to give some history to this story before I get to the actual story. Two springs ago we had a huge flood in the southwest part of Wisconsin. Most of the streams were dramatically affected by this flood. Many streams were widened and others had holes where there were never any.

The water finally receded and I decided to go look at my streams to see if any of them were fishable. Most of the bigger streams were still chocolate milk. I decided to take a look at a couple of my brookie streams. I remembered one stream in particular that I had been fishing with a friend at a huge beaver dam. The beaver dam was still intact.

I remember this outing because my friend Frank had a decent sized brookie on, and all of a sudden the water erupted under the brookie and a huge almost flush of a toilet happened under the brookie. The brookie was sucked under and all of a sudden the pole was bent in half. What ever had the brookie was big and dove towards the bottom. The action ended as quickly as it began. There was the brookie floating on the top of the water. The brookie was still hooked. We brought it in and took a photo of the 10 inch brookie close-up. It had teeth marks the entire length of the fish. We decided it had endured enough injury for the day and popped it back in the beaver dam hole. Frank and I did NOT see the-would be brookie stealer but we both knew it was large.

That beaver dam grew in legend that year. Frank and I went back numerous times and never hooked up on any trout. Not a single trout. It was really odd. Prior to having that brookie almost stolen, we caught many brookies in that area. We finally gave up and decided the brookie stealer had moved on.

This spring we had even a bigger flood. I did my traditional look see after the water went down. Again the bigger streams were dirty and no fishing. The memory of that big fish trying to steal the brookie from Frank came back to me. I knew where I was going. Hello Big Beaver Dam Hole. The floods had completely knocked out the dam. The once 100 yard long and 8 feet deep beaver dam hole was about three feet deep now. I was really disappointed because I figure the Monster of The Beaver Dam has surely moved on.

I walked downstream first and all of the remnants of the beaver dam was down stream. I did a 180 and went up stream. Far in the distance I could see some action on the water. I dismissed it at first as the beavers trying to rebuild their dams. The closer I got....it looked like minnows scurrying in to the shallows with a big wake behind them. It was still a good 80 yards ahead of me. At 40 yards I could see that those weren't minnows in the shallows...They were good sized brook trout and they were being chased into the shallows by an enormous trout. The trout's back was coming out of the water as it chased the brookies into the shallows and ate any of them that got too close. My camera was out and my point and shot digital didn't have a good enough zoom to capture the carnage from this fish. I needed to get closer. I took four more steps and the action turned off. The big fish must have felt me walking trying to get closer.

I told this story to quite a few anglers and they just smiled and nodded their heads and said : "Ya....right...An enormous trout chasing brookies in the shallows." To them it was just too much of a tale to swallow. I tried to talk a couple of them into stalking the trout. They all had better things to do. I tried for this fish minimum fifty times this year. I had not even a whisper of a bite.

About a month later my buddy Joe Chadwick and I went back to the beaver dam to fish. The beavers had repaired their dam and the massive beaver dam was back there in its full glory. Joe and I fished it hard for three hours. No bites. We moved on. We walked back downstream to my truck and took a look at the beaver dam one more time. There was no action. The beaver had made many runs to make entry in to the beaver dam easier. They were hidden in tall weeds. I was leading the way back to the truck. I told Joe to be careful of this one beaver run. Joe must have not heard me and he stepped into the beaver run and tumbled down the bank in to the beaver dam. I asked him if he was OK and he just barked out " Why didn't you tell me there was a run here?" After I stopped laughing at Joe treading water in the huge eight feet deep beaver dam... I noticed a huge wake going up stream. Joe falling in the water had spooked the brookie stealer and now it had shown itself to us again.

Joe and I went back another twenty times to try for the big trout. I always let Joe have the hole first because he said he had discovered the trout by falling in and he should have first crack at it. We did NOT catch anything. Not even a tiny brookie. We decided we needed to try some different tactics. On the way home I told Joe that BIG trout turn in to nocturnal feeders when they get really big. This one fell into the big category. We decided night fishing was in order.

We went back and pruned some of the willows and did some practice casting in the light of day to make sure we could cast properly during the night time hours. The path to the beaver dam was manicured and any holes were noted so we would not fall into them during darkness. We looked for a good battle position on the water's edge and an easy place for netting. We went to *Cabela's* and got two headlamps.

So now... What were we going to use to catch this Leviathan? We decided to be prepared for many ways to tempt this trout. We were going to time our assault on it during the time of the Hex hatch. The Hex were late this year because of the major flooding. A trip to a local fly shop was in order. We got a couple Hex patterns and a couple mouse patterns. We strung up the five weight fly rod with a 3x leader and the Hex emerger pattern. We had heard of hex hatches in the area.

We also got out a spinning rod and put eight pound fireline on it and a size six eagle claw with a small split shot part way up the line. We decided if one method failed we would try the other. I stopped at the local *Kwik Trip* and got a dozen night crawlers and went fishing for chubs. I caught six chubs and cut off their tails about one inch up from the tail. So now we were ready. Night crawlers and chub tails and a readied fly rod. We also had some size nine floater *rapalas* in rainbow color (they don't make brookie color).

The alarm rang at two am. I picked up Joe and off we went for our night time adventure. I parked the truck quite a ways from the normal parking spot. I wanted to have every possible advantage. We walked slowly to the woods edge. I put on my headlamp. I told Joe to leave his off. The approach to the hole seemed like it took an eternity. I turned mine off also quite a ways from the hole. Joe wanted to get right in there with a chub tail. I told him we needed to look and listen for a while. We actually took a seat for about ten minutes. We both looked at each other at the same time. Joe said, "What the heck was that sound?" I told Joe it was a slurp sound. I had read about the sound in many fly fishing magazines. I had never heard the sound myself. We sat there a little longer the sound got closer to our battle station. I handed Joe the fly rod and told him to have at it. There was a hex hatch going on and we had stumbled on it.

It was actually quite intimidating casting in the pitch black. I told Joe to cast towards the slurping sounds. Joe asked me how he would know when to set the hook. I told him to set after he heard the slurp. The first cast in the large beaver dam was off target. Joe put his second cast near the sounds. It seemed almost instant...there it was...the Slurp sound. Joe set it hard.

The fish went directly to the bottom and hunkered down. It did a figure eight a couple times. I don't think it knew it was hooked. Finally it realized it was hooked and it went screaming upstream at Mach 8. There was another small submerged beaver dam up there and I was worried the trout would get entangled in the beaver dam. I yelled at Joe "Turn it!" "Muscle it!" It can't get into the other dam. The reel on the rod was just screaming and the rod was bent in half. Joe was like a deer in the headlights. He froze. He yelled... "Can't control it!"

I told him to take one step into the water and invert the fly rod and stick it directly into the water. I told him to keep the rod bent over. He didn't understand me. He wanted more explanation. I just yelled "Just Do It!" He followed my directions to the letter and the trout turned and came back down stream. Joe was reeling for all his worth. He had it in the main beaver dam again. It was showing no signs of getting tired. It was Joe's turn yell. "Get in the %^43^^7 water and net that fish!" I told him it wasn't ready to be netted. Joe said: "I don't care... Get in there."

I took three steps out and was at the top of my chest waders. I told Joe to get it closer to me so I could net it. The trout swam by me and I made a half hearted netting attempt. I had not even seen the fish yet. I thought I better get a try while it was near me. I tried and I missed. Joe was yelling. "If you cause me to lose this fish I will never talk to you again!" I took one more half step out and the water was even with my waders. I told him he had to get it head up so I could see it to net it. He kind of brought it to the surface. I went deep under the fish and brought it to the surface with the netting action. The trout would not fit in the net from the side and the net got tangled up in the line. I was certain I was going to lose this fish. I dropped the net on purpose and the line came free from the net. I recovered the net. I decided I was going to go in up to my neck and net this thing. I took one big step forward and went deep...almost to my neck and made a lunging deep netting attempt at the fish. I got it in the net by sheer luck. I lifted the net over my head and walked out of the hole. I did NOT know how big the trout was. It felt heavy so I assumed I had scooped up mud with the trout.

When I got to shore I turned on my headlamp. Joe met me at the shore. We just stared in disbelief at what was in the net. A small stream trout in these parts is considered big at 20 inches. This thing was way beyond that. I snapped a couple photos and we measured the male small stream brown trout with a tape measure and a digital scale Joe had brought with. It measured an eye lash over 30 inches and it weighed 10.2 pounds.

THE WIND IN THE TREES

It was late September. I was five years old. I remember the day vividly. It was the day I became a trout angler. I had gone with Dad many times before that year. All of the other times were TRAINING. This is what he called it.

Training entailed many things. One was carrying my dad's extra rod and me constantly asking him: "When will it be my turn to catch a trout?" Dad would always reply: "It will be your turn when you learn the ways of an outdoors man. And one of those ways you haven't learned yet is to be quiet and you need to feel and enjoy your surroundings.

The trout can hear you talking."

At age five my patience and attention span were in the negative numbers. I would lose focus sometimes and pick up sticks and throw them in the water or beat trees with them. My dad would just stare at me and roll his eyes. By the end of that long year of TRAINING... I was ready I thought.

It was late in September. The shadows were long on the water. My dad had me sit down stream side. Dad said: "I want to see if this year of training has sunk in. Tell me what you see and hear." It seemed like a really stupid question to me. Dad said: "We are going to sit here until you tell me what I want to hear."

I thought hard about all the things dad had been saying each time we went out this year. I thought what the heck... I will give it a try. "I see the water. I see the trees. I see the trout on the stringer. I see the BIG trout on the stringer."

Dad gave me that stare and rolled his eyes again. He said: "Have you not learned anything this year? Fishing is like life, if it comes too easy you will not appreciate it. Many times we went fishing this year and caught nothing. Was that an okay outing son?"

Before I could answer. He exclaimed: "Of course it was! Fishing is more than catching BIG fish. It is being out in nature. It is the feel of rain on your face. The smells... Seeing and feeling... The Wind In The Trees. I am not promising you a big trout here. I am not sure we will catch anything, but when we leave here, you will have experienced something special. "Trout fishing... fishing, not catching."

I believe my dad started a little too early in life training me. It never did sink in. I was always amazed at the BIG trout and bummed about the less than fruitful outings. My training was cut short in November of 1967.

My teacher was unable to continue his lessons. Dad died of a heart attack. I was ten.

My fishing trips were alone then. I pedaled my bike out into the country and I tried my best to be just like Dad. I was always after that next big trout. Some of the time I would sit stream side like we used to do... I would look and listen and smell. It just didn't sink in. I had a hard time grasping what my dad had meant.

Adulthood did not change me much. I didn't need the bike now and my trips were farther away and more frequent. On June 3rd 1989 my life changed completely. I married my beautiful wife Barb. My trips to the trout stream became less frequent and they took a serious decline when my daughter Anna was born.

I hurried Anna to become an angler. I took her out at age five to trout fish. She became a mini-me. She was as crazy about the next BIG fish as I was. At age eleven Anna told me that she wasn't going trout fishing with me anymore. She had fished for six years now and it was time to try something else. I was devastated. I had to leave the room when she told me.

I went back in the house later and talked with her momma. I asked Barb what I had done wrong? She said I was a little too intense with Anna and way too critical. Barb told me to give her time and be patient. She would ask me to take her again.

It was the last day of trout season this year. Anna came up to me and asked me if I would take her trout fishing. I was so happy to hear her say it...I had to turn away from her...I got misty eyed.

As we left to go....I thought about what my wife had told me..."too intense...too critical...." I thought back about my training from my Dad. I needed to incorporate those lessons into our outing. I didn't want my only child "Anna" to dislike trout fishing.

We got out of the car and went to stream side....I was about to tell Anna I was sorry and that I would be less intense and would make trout fishing less stressful. Before I opened my mouth with my speech Anna spoke up: "Dad, I really missed trout fishing with you. The smells... the feeling of rain on my face and... The Wind In The Trees."

Male Brook Trout

LIONS, TIGERS AND BEARS

The wilds of Southwestern Wisconsin are home to four different trout. The native species, the brook trout, is actually from the char family and has been here since the beginning. The other residents are either imports or hybrids. The import is the brown trout. Brown trout were brought here in the holds of ships by European settlers. Rainbow trout are not native to the area and are hatchery rejects. The other resident of the area is the "Tiger Trout".

The male brook trout and female brown are the father and mother of the Tiger. The tiger trout is a sterile hybrid cross between a female brown trout and a male brook trout. The fish exhibits unusual markings found in neither parent. Tiger trout are rare in the wild, appearing only in areas where brook and brown trout share spawning grounds. The cross can only happen in one direction. Brown trout sperm can not impregnate brook trout eggs due to being too large. Tiger trout follow the same life cycle as a brook trout and die out in three to five years.

Female Brown Trout

This interspecies cross is unusual, in part because each fish belongs to a separate genus (Salvelinus for brook trout and Salmo for browns). It happens rarely in the wild, but can be (and is) easily performed by fisheries biologists or hatchery technicians.

This wild (non-hatchery) tiger trout was caught in Southwestern Wisconsin. It was caught on a silver panther martin size six by me in Crawford County Wisconsin. The majority of my 13 tigers I have caught have been caught in Crawford County. A typical tiger caught in the wild is between 8 and 16 inches long.

Tigers are pretty fish. The normal vermiculations (wormlike markings) found on the backs of most brookies become enlarged and often contorted into stripes (hence the name 'tiger'), swirls, spots, and rings. The trout also exhibit a greenish cast, which lets you know, when you hook one, that there is something different on the end of your line long before the fish is in hand. Tigers also get their name from their wild abandon when it comes to feeding. Naturally-occurring tiger trout generally appear only in streams that have higher brook trout than brown trout populations. And while they don't appear often, they are becoming more commonly found in the Midwest and New England.

Many states throughout the United States have active stocking programs for tiger trout. Massachusetts, for example. The state record measured 26 inches and weighed 9 pounds, 7 ounces. Angler Michael Shelton caught the fish in Peters Pond, near Sandwich.

Wyoming also boasts an active stocking program. The state-record tiger was caught on July 26, 2006 by Greg Salisbury. It measured 16 1/2 inches long. The lake was stocked the year prior with 12-inch tigers.

Tiger trout were stocked in Wisconsin's Lake Michigan waters between 1974 and 1977, but this stopped due to poor hatch rates in Wisconsin hatcheries. The egg sacs were thin and this made a poor survival rate in fertilized eggs. All tigers caught in Wisconsin these days are the result of natural reproduction. They are not hatchery fish. Lake-run tigers had (and still have) amazing growth rates compared to small stream fish. The world record tiger trout was caught in Lake Michigan on alewives in the middle of the night in 1978. The monster measured over 20 pounds. This is an insane growth rate for four years. Some biologists think it was a blessing in disguise that the tiger were not stocked anymore. They looked at the growth rate and the potential of the tiger trout wiping out many other native species in the Great Lakes and think "What If?"

Wisconsin has a booming population of tiger trout. Many have been caught in the last 12 years in Southwestern Wisconsin. They show no preference for flies or live bait. The best way to find a tiger is to find a stream with a large brook trout population and a stream with many springs. The springs are the key for the water temperatures to be optimal for the hybrid to gestate. Tigers are so rare in Wisconsin, they are not even mentioned in the trout fishing regulations. Most tigers are caught in tiny water and the cover is tight and a small shorter rod is recommended. Happy hunting for your "Tiger" in the wilds of the Wisconsin Driftless Area.

Tiger Trout

(Story appeared in Field & Stream in 2007.)

NASTY

We lived in Milwaukee. My father and mother hated the big city. We lived there because that is where the welding and steam-fitting jobs were plentiful. Dad was born and raised in a small town in northern Wisconsin.

My father left to hunt or fish every chance he got. The trips alternated between Oconto Falls (His hometown) and (Mom's) Gays Mills.

It was the fall of 1958 and our family was in Gays Mills. My dad wanted to go pheasant hunting. My dad and uncle went hunting. The bird hunting was OK that day... The job hunting was even better! On the way home to Milwaukee my dad sprung it on the family.

While pheasant hunting he ran into a guy that worked

at the power plant in Genoa. He was the plant manager. Dad was hired during a pheasant outing to be the new welder there.

My dad was so excited to get out of the big city; he had even bought a house in Gays Mills already. We were moving in two days. The house was 33 steps from the Kickapoo River. It was a four bedroom with a large front and rear porch and a huge yard for the children.

My father went in to his job site and contacted his boss. The boss was not surprised at my dad's leaving. He told dad that "You always left to the sticks every chance you got." "Have a wonderful life in rural Wisconsin." My dad made one more stop before he left his old employ.

It was at the company bulletin board. Dad had seen an ad there. "Puppies" to good home. Beagle and Spaniel mix. My dad had always wanted a hunting dog. He loved grouse/pheasant/rabbit/squirrel hunting and figured now that he had a house, he could have his first dog. Dad stopped on the way home and picked up a puppy.

She was a beagle and spaniel mixture, reddish brown colored with a little wave to her fur on the back. Her original name was Ginger. My oldest sister named her.

Ginger was the ultimate family pet and hunting dog combined. My dad didn't waste any time taking her into the wild to hunt. Her first outing was a rabbit hunt.

Her beagle half was obvious from the get go. She had that beagle bellar.....and stubborn on the track mentality. Dad and Ginger had a wonderful first outing. They harvested three rabbits. It was time to go home to show the family the fruit of their first hunt together...but Ginger was on a hot track.

She was on a rabbit and she wasn't giving up. My dad sat and waited for her by the van for two hours. Every so often he heard a bellar in the distant. He finally got disgusted and went home for reinforcements, leaving Ginger there.

Rabbit hunting was about forty minutes from home. Dad drove home cussing that stubborn dog the entire way. When Dad got home he was met by my two oldest sisters and mom in the driveway. They were worried about Dad and Ginger. Dad was angry at the dog. He was ready to give up on her for not listening properly.

My mom had all the kids load up into the yellow van. Mom and the girls had grown quite fond of the dog and they were going to make Dad go back and get her. We went directly to the rabbit place. My mom even offered to have the girls look for the dog.

Mom explained to Dad, "Do you want a lazy dog or do you want one that stays on track? This was her first time. She needs more training." Dad wasn't angry at the dog by the time we got there. We pulled off the road and went into the woods to look for Ginger.

She must have heard the vehicle...She met us half way into the woods.

She was muddy and wet. Three quarters of her body was covered in burs. She was happy to see Mom and the sisters... When Dad yelled at her. "Ginger get over here!" Ginger cowered and slowly worked her way over to my dad.

Dad grabbed Ginger by the scruff of the neck and lifted her nose to nose with him and he yelled at her as loud as he could. "When I say come I mean come!" He picked her up and carried her back to the yellow van.

Everyone was quiet on the way home. We were afraid that Dad was so angry at Ginger that he might give her away. Dad told all of us NOT to pet the dog. Not to show any attention to her the entire way home. We were all certain that Dad was going to give her away the next day.

We all piled out of the van. Dad told my oldest sister it was her job to clean up the dog. He said she was NASTY and she wasn't allowed in the back porch until she was completely clean. It took my two sisters three hours to clean her up.

The next morning my dad woke us all up and we had a family meeting. We were all certain that Dad called the meeting to tell us he was giving away the dog. The girls were all crying and my mom was a little misty-eyed. My dad announced that the he was keeping the dog... but he had decided to change her name. Her name from that day forward would be NASTY. He made it clear to us that if the dog didn't listen to him, she would be gone.

Nasty turned into the best hunting dog ever. My dad said that she was better than any AKC dog. She listened and stayed on a hot trail better than any 500 dollar AKC over priced dog.

I remember the rituals before hunting. My dad fired up the dog by going to the gun cabinet. He would open up the cabinet and then close it and walk away. It was a game my dad liked to play with the dog. He would work her into a fever pitch. She would get so fired up by the time Dad put on the hunting coat...She would be howling and running round the house bouncing off of furniture. Mom would finally get sick of the two and kick them out of the house.

They would get into the yellow van and go hunting.

As I got older I yearned to go with them. At age eight I was allowed to go. The three of us made many hunting memories together. I can still remember like yesterday the time Nasty had a squirrel latch on to her nose after my dad had shot it. She shook it off and let it lay. She did not attack it. Dad had taught her well about not chewing up game.

Then there was the time that Dad winged a pheasant and it jumped into the Kickapoo River to get away from the dog. Nasty did NOT hesitate. She jumped right off the eight foot sheer bank and swam and retrieved the rooster. We had to slide down the bank and help her up the bank. She did NOT drop the bird.

She always came along on fishing outings too. She sat right along side my dad in the back of the boat. She could sense our excitement when we had a nice fish on and bark like crazy. My dad didn't like it at first but got used to it and called it our **"Cheering Section"**. She also came along trout fishing but kept her distance behind us as to not spook the trout.

Nasty did not understand deer hunting. Dad went to the gun cabinet quietly. He tried to sneak out of the house without her seeing. He loaded up the yellow van in the dark. Nasty always watched at the window. She was waiting her turn to be loaded in the van. Dad left without her. She would lay by the gun cabinet sulking the entire time he was gone. I would tease her a little before Dad actually came home. I would act excited and say Dad was home. She fell for it a couple times and smartened up quickly because she did not hear the van coming. My mom would get mad at me for teasing the dog. She told me that

Nasty loved Dad and humans could learn a lesson from her on "**unconditional love**".

Nasty would always be the first one to know Dad was home from deer hunting. She would hear the van before we could see it. She would let out a howl and be bouncing off of the front door to greet my dad upon his return.

She quickly forgot about deer hunting and was allowed to ride in the yellow van again. She had her position. She staked the claim to the front seat long before I was old enough to hunt. My place was the next row on the van and Nasty and Dad in the front. The dog always had to have the window open so she could have her head out the window while we drove places.

Many falls had come and passed. Nasty had developed a white muzzle and was getting a little slower...but she still had that fire burning for hunting. November came and it was her worst time of the year. Dad was going hunting without her again. At least I was home to play with. Once I tried to teach her to fetch a stick. She just stared at me with her big brown eyes. She cocked her head to the side and I swear if she could talk she would have been saying: "That is a stick, fool, I am not that dumb." We spent many hours waiting for Dad together. I wasn't old enough to go deer hunting yet.

Nasty slept in front of the gun cabinet. She waited for her human to come home. It was the last night of deer season. About ten pm. Nasty let out her "Dad is Home Howl." We all went out side to the yellow van. Things were a little different this year for Nasty.

Her human never came in the house and the yellow van left without her again. What Nasty didn't know was that her human had died while deer hunting of a heart attack. November 23, 1967.

Nasty didn't have closure like we did. We went to Dad's funeral and got to say goodbye to him. She waited for many days for the yellow van to come home. She would stand on her hind legs and look out the window at vehicles that went by. She slept in front of the gun cabinet.. The yellow van didn't come. We had sold the yellow van to my uncle. My uncle wanted to have his brother's hunting vehicle.

Nasty finally quit looking out the window. I wasn't old enough to take her hunting. My uncle wanted to have her. My mother said she was part of the family and was staying where she belonged. Nasty became kinda fat. She was a family dog now. Not a hunting dog anymore. The years passed slowly for her.

It was June of 1972. My sister was getting married. My Uncle had asked if he could give away my sister. He was my dad's only brother so my mother and sister agreed.

My uncle was supposed to arrive the day before at noon. Nasty went crazy at about 11:15am. She was howling and bouncing off the front screen door. She tore her way through the screen door. She heard her yellow van coming .

Her human was finally coming home.

Nasty was the first to meet the yellow van in the driveway. She went directly to the driver's door. My uncle got out. She immediately jumped in the van. She searched the entire van.. My uncle left the van door open. Nasty stayed in the van in the passenger seat. She sat there for a couple hours before Mom went outside and brought her into the house. Nasty went to her place in front of the gun cabinet and laid down.

We all greeted my uncle and the hours flew by. The next thing I knew we were watching my sister leave the church and we were all throwing rice. It was about eight pm when we all got home. It was quiet in the house.

There was no Nasty at the door to greet us as usual.

I went upstairs looking for her. There she was asleep in front of the gun cabinet. I bent down to pet her and... it was obvious she wasn't sleeping. She had died. I didn't want to ruin the day's happening and tell everyone about Nasty. I quietly carried her to back porch and gave her a kiss good bye on the top of the head. I wrapped her in one of her favorite blankets and put her in a wooden box that my dad used for reloading equipment. I placed one of Dad's hunting caps and a squirrel call in with her.

Everyone was still up talking. I got the keys to the car and put Nasty in the car. It was clear where I was going. I carefully cut out the sod and dug a hole and replaced the sod carefully. I said my goodbye to my childhood companion . Now Nasty could rest in peace.

She was with her HUMAN.

THE HEART OF THE DRIFTLESS AREA

When people think about Wisconsin, they think about cheese, dairy cows, and the Green Bay Packers. Few people equate the Badger State with trout fishing but it has a cold climate, gets lots of snow, and the southwestern corner, which is part of the Driftless Area, is laced with limestone streams. It's a coldwater fishery seemingly created by geologic forces for the purpose of holding trout. And today, it's so full of trout that many of the anglers who come here leave with a different notion of Wisconsin.

For example, I'm friends with famed college-basketball coach Bobby Knight. He and I met through a mutual friend eight years ago, and I guided him on some of the rivers in the Driftless Area. I had followed his career for decades as he set the NCAA record for wins during tenures at Indiana University and Texas Tech. Since meeting him and guiding him those years ago, he's been back here six times. Coach Knight's passion for basketball is rivaled by his passion for fly fishing, and he's as particular about where he fishes as he is about properly running the motion offense. "I've fished rivers all over the world—from Russia to Bozeman and everywhere in between—and this area rivals any of those places," he says.

The area Coach Knight refers to is known as the Driftless Area, and it is a large section of land that covers parts of four states—most of it in Wisconsin with smaller swaths in Minnesota, Iowa, and Illinois. The area holds trout in each state except Illinois. In Wisconsin, the DA extends from the southwestern most corner of the state along the Mississippi River and hugs the river shore all the way up to Buffalo County. It extends as far east as the town of Spring Green.

The term *driftless* comes for the word *drift* and its association with glacial activity. The area of Wisconsin that exhibits *drift* consists of boulders and scrapings from a glacier. The absence of such boulders and scrapings means a lack of drift. In short, the Driftless Area escaped a good scrubbing in the Midwest's last glacial period, which ended about 10,000 years ago, and the rolling hills and hidden valleys of modern-day southwestern Wisconsin were left untouched.

One reason the glaciers skirted this area is that limestone, known as karst, was not suitable for lubricating the glacier, so the glacier went another route until it melted, flowed in to this non-glaciated landscape, and cut deep in to the limestone, leaving behind many small and large streams and rivers. This same karst is what makes the spring creeks of the area perfect for trout. The groundwater is filtered by the limestone, which purifies the water and funnels it to the aquifer or water table at ideal cold temperatures. The groundwater seeps in to the streams from the multitude of springs in the area. The constant temperature of the springs in the area remains around 52 degrees, which helps keep the streams cool in the summer and not too cold in the frigid Wisconsin winters, allowing trout to thrive.

Lots of Trout Water

The three main waterways in Driftless Area are the Mississippi, Wisconsin, and Kickapoo rivers. The Mississippi is the westernmost border that drains the Wisconsin and the Kickapoo. Every small stream or tributary of the area dumps into or feeds one of these three rivers.

"While these are the three main waterways, the trout fishing is best in the many miles of tributaries. The Wisconsin and Mississippi Rivers are just too warm to sustain trout year around. The main branch of the Kickapoo has browns in it but the best fishing is in those tributaries and they are concentrated in four counties in the extreme southwestern Wisconsin."

Wildcat Mountain State Park near Ontario, Wisconsin has 3,603 acres interlaced with outstanding trails and camping areas with miles and miles of trout streams running through it. The Kickapoo Valley Reserve is just below Wildcat Mountain State Park and it has 8,569 acres of unspoiled lands run by the state of Wisconsin and the Ho Chunk Nation and is just north of LaFarge, Wisconsin. The reserve has the Kickapoo River running its entire length. The main branch of the Kickapoo River in the Reserve has brown trout . The water temperatures there are cold enough for browns but are inadequate for brook trout. It is more common for the trout to be in the smaller tributaries and at the confluences of the smaller streams and the Kickapoo River.

In the heart of the Driftless Area is Crawford County, which has 293 miles of designated trout water. Vernon County, just north of Crawford, has two state parks. The state parks are loaded with trout streams. All the streams in the state parks are open to the public. The entire county of Vernon has 503 miles of trout streams. Richland County is just east of these counties and holds more than 267 miles of designated trout water. Farther south, and south of the Wisconsin River, Grant County has 206 miles of trout streams. That adds up to over 1,269 miles of designated trout streams in four counties. The heart of fly fishing is the joy of exploration and discovery. With 1,269 miles of streams in the area you could not fish all of them in a lifetime. Some of those streams are two feet wide while others may be thirty feet wide. These are only the designated trout streams. Every trickle over twelve inches deep in the area holds trout. Timber Coulee Creek in Vernon County boasts more than 6,000 trout per mile.

Here are some good starting points in each county for your adventures in each county. Crawford County has a huge stretch of public water on Pine Creek at State Highway 179 and Duha Ridge Road. If you enter at the bridge on State Highway 179, you can fish upstream on Pine Creek for a couple miles. This stretch is all eased and relatively easy walking. Willow Creek in Richland County near Lloyd has excellent fishing. You can park at Hollow Road and fish all the way up and through Lloyd.   In Grant County, Castle Rock Creek has one of the longest-standing catch-and-release-only stretches in the state. This are was established in 1977. The boundaries of the area has fluctuated over the years but it has been "*Catch and Release* Only" since 1977. Thirty inch browns are not uncommon in this water. This stretch is clearly marked with Public Fishing Signs and there are public parking lots to assist you on where to begin. Castle Rock Creek is 98 percent "Artificial Only and Catch and Release Only". There is a tiny section in the middle that is catch and keep and bait is allowed. This area is marked with signs at the beginning and end of the section. The stream is located at

Church Road on County Trunk Q. The county's fish manager stocks the Castle Rock with huge brooders from the local hatcheries. The only problem with Castle Rock is it dirties very easily and takes a long time to clear after even a small rainfall. Vernon County's biggest waterway is the West Fork of the Kickapoo River. All you need to do is find the village of Avalanche on County Trunk S and the campgrounds there, and you are in trout heaven.

The Wisconsin Inland trout season always opens the first Saturday in March and closes the last Sunday in April. The early season requires anglers to use artificials only, and catch and release is mandatory. The season reopens the first Saturday in May and runs through the end of September. The regulations during the second season vary. Second season opens for bait and harvest. This is not true in all areas. The streams actually sometimes flip flop back and forth on the same streams. Some stretches are artificial only and no harvest and then you could walk upstream a couple miles and then there is sign that changes to harvest. These areas are clearly marked. There are not many of these midstream changes . You will need to refer to the Trout Pamphlet to stay abreast of regulations. You will receive the pamphlet when you purchase a license.

Wisconsin has hundreds of miles of easements on the streams. Easements are agreements that the state has made with landowners to allow public access. This means that public access is allowed through private property. These easements do not cover the entirety of the land. It only gives the public a through fare stream side. These easements are clearly marked at bridges and entry points. The locals are friendly and will give you permission 99 percent of the time if asked. If you can't find a land owner, Wisconsin has a unique law that allows for wading on water that flows through private land if you enter the water at a bridge or other public access. The Trout Pamphlet explains the wading law in detail.

The weather conditions in the spring can vary quite a bit. If you come during the early season, long johns and layers of warm clothing is a must. Temperatures on the March opener can get down to single digits, and there could be two feet of snow on the ground. The weather is very unpredictable. I have seen April afternoons where I have fished in short sleeves and the caddis hatch is unbelievable, and others when the temperatures dipped below freezing. Don't let a little snow and cold scare you away, though. The blue-winged olives hatch and you will know it by the number of them you'll see on the snow.

The trout are very weather sensitive here, and the different hatches vary due to temperature and season changes. Your fishing tactics need to change with the weather. Many people fish small stuff in Wisconsin's early season. The trout have specific caloric needs in colder water and usually won't move for small offering. Their metabolism is in low gear and in cold water the trout school up in wintering holes. These holes are typically the deepest holes in the area with slack current on the bottom so they can easily hold in place.

An early season big trout-getter is a size 6 Hornberg on a long leader. I find an indicator is helpful for detecting very subtle hits in the early season. Place the indicator about two feet deeper than the water's depth. A small piece of soft tungsten about 12 inches up from the fly keeps the offering where it needs to be. Down low and slow is critical during Wisconsin's early season. Weighted Bunny or Turkey Leeches in size 8 and 10 are deadly also.

Hexagenia limbata, the second-largest mayfly species in the United States, hatches here from the middle of June until early July. The hatch is temperature-dependent, and most often happens at night in a stream with a silty bottom. The hatch can be very heavy, as bridges in are sometimes covered with mayflies and need to be plowed with snow-removal equipment to make them passable. There are times mayflies can even be seen on weather radar because the hatches are so huge.

A stout leader on a 5- or 6-weight rod with a backbone and night lamps are a must during these periods. The huge browns come out to binge during the evening, and a keen ear and good set if timing for setting the hook when you hear the *slurp* is vital. Browns over 20 inches are not uncommon during the *Hex* hatch. The Hex Emerger pattern is the go-to fly that turns on the sleeping giants and they lose their inhibitions and sip or slurp these huge flies until they are full.

The dog days of late July to the middle of August brings higher stream temperatures, and the fishing slows down and so do the anglers. As the hot days wind down, the hoppers come out and the action on terrestrials can be wicked.

In recent years fish managers have been instrumental in the reviving the population of native brook trout. Efforts to improve the stock and conditions around the streams have helped boost trout populations.

This region is managed mainly by Dave Vetrano, who has been instrumental in the stream born-stocking initiative. Brook trout were nearly extinct in the area streams before the stream born stocking program. These fry and adults are collected from Ash Creek and east branch of Mill Creek in Richland County.

It is not uncommon to catch a 14-inch brook trout in the area. A 100-brook trout day is well within your grasp. A 7-foot 6-inch 3-weight rod is the proper tool for the job. The brook trout are not terribly selective and you can really have a memorable outing. A go-to local fly that is a must for brookies and browns is the Pink Squirrel, created by local fly-fishing legend John Bethke.

The focus on stream-born stocking and non-hatchery reared brook and brown trout have caused natural reproduction to take off in many of the local streams. Hatchery-reared trout have a different gestation period and hatch out too early, at a time when there is little forage in the river, and they wind up starving in the frigid water. Stocking stream-born fry takes care of this problem. The hatchery fish and the stream-born fish intermingle, and eventually they produce fry that hatch when chances of survival are optimal.

Farming practices have gotten better in this region too, and the Wisconsin Department of Natural Resources has made many policies to protect the streams from runoff. The most notable is the bank restoration effort. When the Wisconsin Department Of Natural Resources purchases easements, it also incorporates language in the easements that allows for bank stabilization. Large boulders are placed in stream and along banks that have began to erode. The banks are seeded and tapered to stop the runoff. Runoff from local farms not only adds fertilizer, natural and chemical, to the water but also increases water temperatures. According to my own temperatures readings, the stream temperatures for the entire area have gone down an average of six degrees over the last eight years.

The rebirth of the brook trout population has led to some overlap between populations of brookies and brown trout. With the overlap, some male brook trout have found brown redds and fertilized them, and the results are tiger trout. There are stocking programs in many states for tiger trout but there are no stocking of tigers in Wisconsin. Stream-born tigers are very rare. They are the "mules" of the trout world, and this is a natural hybrid and can only go one way: The brook trout is always the father. Brown - trout sperm are too big to impregnate brook trout eggs. The heart of the Driftless Area boasts a thriving population of stream-born tigers, which have voracious appetites and show wild abandon when attacking a fly.

Pack your gear and be ready for a serious treat. The streams in the area are calling your name. You will have the streams to yourself. That is if you don't count the dairy cows and turkeys. I have fished the area streams for 48 years. Fishing in the area has never been better. When anglers reminisce, they often talk about the good old days. Well, the good old days are right now in the Driftless Area.

(Story featured in American Angler Magazine in July/August 2010)

DANCING WITH TROUT

It was opening day 2003. My friend John Armstrong drove up to Wisconsin to fish with me. John is a Pennsylvania angler displaced a couple times over due to job changes.

John called me four times on the way up and interrogated me about the weather conditions. The four degree weather up here was really not very inviting to a Georgia native.

John and I have been fishing "buds" for quite some time. He used to manage Madison Outfitters on Madison's west side. His wife works for Oscar Mayer. One fine day in September 2002, John's wife was moved to the Atlanta office. To make a long story short; John had to drive eleven hours to fish with me now. John has done that at least once a year since his move.

John rolled in the Friday night and we prepared for fishing. I was amazed at how many pairs of long underwear John had brought with him. He was going to wear 2 pairs along with fleece wader liners. I told him he would look like the little brother from *The Christmas Story* movie after he geared up, the one with the *Red Rider* BB gun   theme. I wondered if he would even be able to put his arms to his sides.

We hit the stream at eight am. We parked his truck at the beginning of the area and we planned on fishing about two miles up to a very deep hole. I called the final hole the sewer hole. It had a large spillway and was the first obstruction on that waterway. It was a perfect wintering hole.

We were having fair luck and John could put his arms to his sides. I still tormented him and kept saying. "You'll shoot your eye out with that thing." The temperature did not get warmer and the robin's egg blue sky didn't help at all. We were cleaning ice out of the eyes about every other cast.

John had never fished this stretch before and was growing weary due to the slippery banks and excessive clothing. I told him we would go back to the truck after we fished the last hole on the stretch. The last hole always held a big one.

The end was in sight. John saw the hole and thanked me for not letting him turn back. He had a little more spring in his step now and the prospect of a big trout was very real. John said he needed to change his leader and his entire set up. He wasn't walking all this way to hook a big one and have it school him. I watched as John put a new 11-foot leader on. He was using 3x before but switched to 4x here with an indicator.

John's rig had a size six hornberg on the end. John

made sure there was a new leader without tippet tied to it. There is moldable tungsten placed above the fly about 12 inches. Tungsten, not a split shot. John said. The split would cause a nick in the line and a decent trout would break off. The last part of the rig was a bright orange stick on strike indicator at eight feet up the line.

We made the battle plan. John was out in the water to about his knees. He was hesitant to go any farther due to the extreme cold conditions. He had the left lane of the hole. I was to block the trout if he got one on that would try to escape out the right side of the hole.

John is a pretty good caster and had his hornberg up in the sweet spot below the spill in short order. John explained to me that because of the cold the trout would be on the bottom holding tight and any fast action by the fly would be ignored. John called it the dredging method. John even paused a couple times for long periods during the retrieve.

I can remember it like yesterday. John is at the end of his retrieve and just taking the fly out of the water. He is telling me he calls the last part of the retrieve the most important. In cold weather conditions like these when he takes the fly out he does what he calls a "Shake and Bake". The action mimics a bait fish swimming to the surface. It is a slow upward lift of the fly and pauses and stutter shakes are used as the fly exits the water. It was a very slow meticulous dance to entice the trout.

John is an excellent teacher. He is looking right at me when he is talking and explaining the Shake and Bake. He just had told me how important it is to watch the fly come out of the water because lots of times a big one will hit it at the very last moment as it breaks the surface. John readjusted his view on the fly as he did the final lift.

It was like it was choreographed to happen. John slowly did his Dance and the surface erupted as his fly hit the surface. The surface was alive with a big trout directly at John's feet that had NOT been tired out by a battle. The trout was on about four feet of line and giving all it had to escape from its captor. It got off the surface for a moment and tried to dive and run out the side of the hole. John reached for his net and did a right side step all at once. He lunged at the trout with his net fully extended. The only problem was that to John's right was about three feet deeper and when John side stepped his right foot found nothing but deep water and John fell over like a tree.

It happened in slow motion it seemed. There was John with that nice brown in his net and he stood up out of the water and one side of his body was wet and I could see the ice forming already on his clothing. John was shaking uncontrollably but still wanted a photo taken of the trout and him. One photo and off we went on a full jog back to truck.

We were about 150 yards back towards the truck and we came up to a dairy farm. We were talking all the way. John din't know if he could make it all the way back to the truck being wet. I suggested to find a dairy farmer and warm up in his house or maybe John should find a warmer place in the barn and I would run and get the truck. Luck was with us a little this day and we found a farmer right away and he gave us a ride to John's truck. We sat in the guy's truck for a while so John's truck could warm up.

Out John hopped and went directly to the back of his truck to his bin that had his extra clothing and long johns in them. John stripped down to his birthday suit right there on the roadway and put on warm clothing. The farmer bid us a fond farewell and John and I looked at my digital camera while he sat in his truck and warmed up. I can remember him saying. "I sure the heck hope you got a good photo of that trout with all the DANCING I had to do." The photo turned out perfectly and we were fishing again twenty minutes later.

Later that night I can remember us sitting in a local watering hole and reliving the experience and sharing the photo with the bar patrons. John said at the end of the night: "This is what it is all about. "Fishing with good friends, catching big trout, sitting around talking smart with whoever will listen...AND *"Dancing with Trout."*

ONLY ONE DAY

As a young pup I was left to explore and to make my way on my own a lot. My sisters were quite a handful for my mother to keep track of. They ranged from age 3 to age 17. They were toddlers and young women. All of the problems of youth wrapped up in a single parent family. My mother had been recently been left a widow at age 39 with six children.

At times I almost felt like a leaf in the wind. I was making lots of decisions alone without any adult supervision. Many of my choices were quite poor looking back in retrospect. I am actually quite lucky to still be on this earth with some of the foolish choices I made.

Not all of my choices were foolish. It was late fall and trout season was closed so I was limited in the things I could do. When I got bored I thought of things that could make me money. I decided to search the path from the high school to the downtown area and look in the ditch along the path and pick up pop bottles. In those days you could get two cents a bottle and usually one trip on this path gave me at least fifty pop bottles. It doesn't seem much now but a DOLLAR was a big deal to me back then.

I started on Main Street and worked towards the high school. The pop bottle spelunking was going quite well and I had to go home quickly and get a bag because there were just too many to carry. The ditch was a veritable gold mine this day and I was weighed down heavily with at least sixty pop bottles on the end of my journey.

I was already thinking about what I was going to spend my HUGE pay day on. I had the bag hung over my shoulder and was walking back to the grocery store to cash in my treasure and I saw two high school students dressed really oddly walking towards the high school.

I was the curious type and asked what was up with the costumes. The two girls said they were going to be in a play called "Brigadoon" at the High School later that night and they were heading there to do their final dress rehearsal. They asked me if I wanted to come watch them practice their lines. I immediately said "NO"; I thought it wasn't manly enough for me to be interested in. I was also in a hurry to cash in my bottles and get some candy or a new fishing lure. I met four more of the cast on the way to the store. They were also walking to the high school and were decked out in costume. These were guys and it really looked like they were getting into their parts. They were practicing their lines as they walked. I was on a mission so I went onward to the grocery store.

I cashed in my grand total of seventy pop bottles and asked the clerk at the store what the play was about. She gave me the short version of the play. It was about a magical place. It was about going back in time to a simpler way of life. The place only appeared once every one hundred years. The name of the play was *"Brigadoon."* I checked out at the store. I bought no candy that day; I bought a spinner to trout fish with in spring. It was getting dark so I decided to go home for supper.

The house was full with activity and the table was already set. My sisters were helping my mom with supper and I was really dirty from all of the ditch diving. My mom sent me to the bathroom to shower and put clean clothing on. I protested but I always listened to my mom.

The rest of the family was already seated when I returned. I sat down and ate supper. The topic of the play at the high school came up and my mother gave me a few more details about the play. It sounded really interesting and I thought what the heck. My mom made me take a shower and put on clean clothes. Why waste it, I thought. I had a quarter left from ditch diving and that is what it would cost to get in the play. Off I went to the play.

The opening of the play had a couple hunters wandering in the mist and they seemed quite lost. The special effects in 1968 were amazing. They must have used dry ice or something similar. The stage was engulfed in mist. At eleven years old I internalized much of what I saw and heard. These hunters became people in my life. One of them was my Dad and he was lost and couldn't find his way home from hunting in northern Wisconsin.

My Dad had died about a year ago while deer hunting. I still had this weird fantasy that he didn't really die and that he would appear at home one day. I was swept away by the story of play from the moment I saw the lost hunters. I watched the play on the edge of my seat the entire time. I was glad that it was dark in the gym because I was fighting back tears quite often. I loved that play and it is my all time favorite. However, I didn't like the ending of the story, because you would have to wait another hundred years for Brigadoon to reappear.

The play touched me because it talked about simpler times and going back into your past. I remember all of the things my Dad taught me about the outdoors. I had my own little Brigadoon every time I went to the trout stream. It was where my Dad seemed the happiest and I could imagine him being with me on every outing. Every wildflower he had identified for me reminds me of the magic of the outdoors. All of the smells and sounds of the outdoors take me back.

I can still see him smile when he showed me the **Impatiens balsamina** wildflower. My face must have showed astonishment and awe when he had me touch that orange odd looking flower. I can remember him making sure that I was really close so I could see the flower as the pod area exploded and shot seeds raining down on me. I can not go by a *Touch Me Not* flower in the fall without getting close to it and see my father's smile each time I touch those magical flowers.

MUDDY BOOTS

I need to give a little background to begin the story. Recently I have been doing lots of presentations at schools to encourage young people to take up fishing. Along the way I was asked to speak at some nursing homes also. I have spoke at five now and have a couple more scheduled. My wife used to work at a nursing home and she thought it was a good thing for the retired folks. She called it bringing the trout stream to them.

I spoke at a nursing home this morning. The place I was to speak was the chapel area. I always go early to my presentations to make sure everything is set up properly. When I arrived today I went directly to the chapel. The power point equipment was all set up. There was one resident in the chapel. Her name was Alma. She was quite talkative and she gave me some family history.

Alma started out talking to me complaining that my presentation was getting in the way of her time to pray. I explained to her that I was giving a presentation about trout fishing. She said: "I had my fill of anything fish related from my husband." He died twelve years ago. He was a crazy fisherman. He went out every moment he could go fishing. Alma told me "No thanks" and she wasn't going to sit in on the fishing show.

I really wanted her to see my presentation. I told her that it wasn't only about fishing. There were wildflowers and many beautiful outdoor photos in the show. I worked on her for about twenty minutes and she finally gave in. She shared with me why she had such a dislike for fishing. When she and her husband were first married they were kind of poor. They lived on wild game and anything that swam.

Her husband Albert would come home from fishing and walk all over the house with his muddy boots. Fishing meant relaxation for Albert but it meant work for her. She would have to clean the house after his nonsense. He cleaned the fish right on the kitchen counter and made one heck of a mess. Alma was always happy when he brought home trout instead of pike because pike meant scales and they were all over the kitchen. He cleaned them and she would always have to follow behind him and clean the sink and the floors.

By the time he was done cleaning the fish and traipsing outside he was tired and he would just put those muddy boots anywhere he pleased. Fishing equaled to mess in her mind. He had asked her numerous times to go along with him. She had gone with him a couple times when they were first married. It just wasn't her cup of tea. Fishing meant wood ticks and usually she ended up muddy and wet.

She said she ate so many fish through the years she thought she might even grow fins. Alma was a tough sell and was sneering most of the first few moments of my presentation. I directed my attention to the other residents that were watching and made eye contact with them more than Alma. About half way through the presentation I noticed something really odd. Alma's facial expression had changed to a big smile and she was hanging on each word and photo. Near the end she changed her facial expression again. She was wiping away tears and the aides asked her if she wanted to go back to her room. She responded with a resounding "NO".

My presentation was over and she sat there a while as I straightened things up and helped put away some chairs. I went over and sat by her and we talked again. She was still weepy. She asked if I had any more fishing stories I would share with her. I talked to her until it was time for her to go to lunch. She thanked me for coming and aides were wheeling her away and she looked me right in the eye and tears were flowing and she said: "What I wouldn't give for just one more time to clean up that old fool's muddy boots from my kitchen floor."

Lenny Harris Senior

A TROUT ANGLER

by: Len Harris, Jr.

Lenny Harris was a family man with five daughters and one son. He loved the outdoors and though his daughters showed no interest in learning the ways of a woodsman, Lenny was blessed with an anxious pupil in his son, "Len Jr."

Junior began his training at an early age, his father taking the time to bring him squirrel and pheasant hunting, northern fishing, long trips in the small rowboat to check bank poles and along on Dad's favorite outdoor pastime, trout fishing. Following his father up the streams like a caddy, Junior toted whichever rod Dad wasn't using, be it the "new fangled spinning rod" or the old bamboo fly rod. Behind Father isn't always the easiest place for a five year old to be; it doesn't take much water to come up to his chest. Whether on the bank, or in the stream, Junior was oft reminded, "Keep the tips out of the trees, and the reels out of the water." Many trips the boy yearned to use the poles he carried, watching his father Lenny catch trout after trout. Countless epic battles were etched into his memory before that fateful day, the day Len Jr. was to become a trout angler.

Not wanting his son's first trout to be a "gimme," or an easy fix, Lenny scouted hard for the right place for his son to experience trout fishing. He wanted this day to be special, he thought, "Too easy, and it won't mean anything to the boy." He decided on a long deep hole, not crowded by too many overhanging trees; a hole the locals called "booger gut." It was perfect.

The way was long and hard; they marched over hill and dale, wading here, through high grass and thick willows there, Junior always taking care with the rods, handling them the way his father had shown him. Timed for the late afternoon, the moment found them heading westward. The late afternoon sun laid long shadows on the water.. The young boy tired, and wanted to quit, asking his father, "Can we go home now?" "No, it's just a little farther. Enough carrying, today is your turn. **Time for you to catch a trout."**

Little Len's eyes lit up and a surge of energy overtook him, the "little farther" seemed like an eternity. Then the willows parted and "the hole" was there for both to see. The young one began to get giddy, and Father sat him down explaining, "Fishing is like life, if it comes too easy you will not appreciate it. I am not promising you a big trout here. I am not sure we will catch anything, but when we leave here, you will have experienced something special. Trout fishing. Fishing, not catching."

Because he had scouted the water, Lenny knew that fish schooled at the head of the pool. He had seen trout working it in the previous outings there. The two sat and watched the pool, teaching young Len this was something special, something to be savored, something unhurried. He had watched his father catch countless trout and carried those same trout for miles on the stringer, a stringer that today already suspended many nice trout. The biggest was an "18" brown trout that Junior had been admiring all day. Getting more and more anxious, he thought: "Now it is my turn to put a trout on that stringer."

His father, wisely deciding that a fly rod would be too difficult for a five year old, handed Junior the spinning rod. "Len, which lure do you want to use?" There was no doubt in Junior's mind he wanted to use the same one Father had used to catch the big one. "Ok Len, get it out of the box and tie it on." Junior retrieved the spinner from its resting place in the box and took care to tie it on exactly like he had been taught. It was a small French spinner, a Mepps with a red bead, a brass bead, a brass blade and no tail. Little Len checked the knot, and bit off the tag end, just like his dad.

The boy had been taught to cast the spinning rod already, but Father was worried about his casting into tight cover, and asked, "Is it ok if I cast the first one for you?" The youngster didn't want to be a baby, having his dad cast for him, but the father persuaded him, saying, "Let me cast the first couple times for you, then you can do it yourself." Junior always listened to his father.

Lenny cast the spinner upstream of the hole, and handed the rod to his son. "Keep the rod tip up, and if the fish is taking drag, stop reeling or you will ruin the reel and lose the fish. Now, you may not catch any fish, but later, when you get older, there will be lots of trout for you to remember."

It was barely ten cranks of the reel handle later, and the trout hit. Junior did not need to set the hook like he had seen his father do so many times, the trout was crazy, swimming upstream like its tail was on fire.

"DAD, DAD" the youngster shouted, "ITS GOING TO PULL THE ROD OUT OF MY HANDS!"

To which his father calmly replied, "Hang on, keep the rod tip high and don't reel."

The trout came about and charged right at them. "Reel in and reel fast, tip up." The trout turned, and danced side to side staying deep within the pool, finally running straight under the bank. The line stopped throbbing.

"I think I lost it, Dad."

Lenny explained to his son, "The fish has buried itself in the bank. Let's try to get it out of there. Grab your line and back up two or three feet, holding the line tight. If it takes off again, let go right away."

The trick worked, and the trout put up two more long runs before surrendering to the boy. "Let it tire some more before you bring it in. Keep constant pressure and reel when you can. Don't horse it." Junior followed the instructions, but the fish came easily toward shore. Both fishermen were eager to see the fish, and it obliged, surfacing not twenty feet from them. The two responded in unison, "Oh my gosh, it is huge." After seeing its potential captors, the fish resumed fighting for its life.

"Stay right there, and keep the tip up high," Senior waded into the pool up to his chest, and netted the fish. He pulled the net close to his chest, trapping the trout, or rather the half of it that fit, in the net. He quickly waded out, placed the fish near Junior and said, "Unhook it. It will be a fine addition to our stringer." The boy proudly unhooked it, put it on the stringer, and marched it back to the car. The trip passed in an instant.

The father and son took a moment to take pictures of the day's catch. Junior had to stand on the picnic table to get at a level where he could take Dad's picture, then off to the gas station, to show off the spoils of the day. The locals wowed about the largest fish on the stringer, a brown trout, some 23 and ¾ inches long, as measured by a plumber with a folding wooden yardstick. Next it was home to show the womenfolk, none of whom believed little Len had caught the fish, (and didn't care much about fishing anyway, it was for boys). Little Len couldn't wait to get the pictures back from the shop; he couldn't wait to show them off. He carried one with him for two years, until it finally gave out and fell apart.

I was looking through some old photographs and came across the picture of my dad, holding those fish. Even though this happened 50 years ago, the memories were as strong as if it had happened just yesterday. I was there again, walking through the streams of southern Wisconsin with my dad.

Lenny Harris left behind a family of six children and one wonderful wife (Jane). Jane steered the Harris ship for many years alone and all of the Harris children moved on to adulthood because of the wonderful job my mom had done. Both of the rods and a photo of my dad with that stringer adorn the wall of my living room. (1961) The photo hangs on the wall at my mother's home also.

I Miss You Dad...

Thank You Mom.

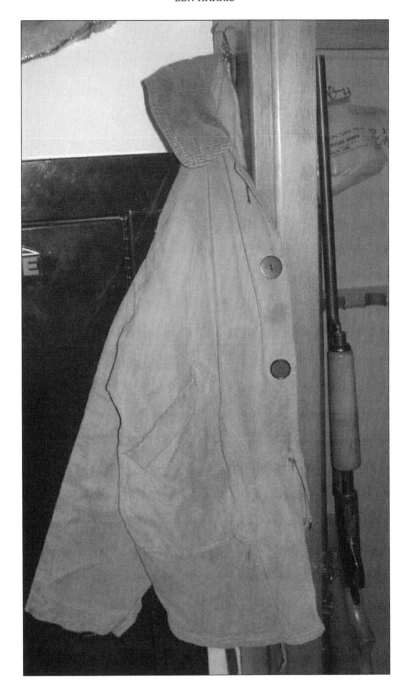

His Old Coat

It is a classic. It has padded shoulder and many pockets for game and shells. Inside the pockets there are memories. The memories of years past and years to come were in those pockets. The coat is stained and tattered. A couple buttons were even missing.

As a young boy I always waited for my father to announce we were going hunting. Usually our dog Ginger gave out the first alarm when my dad took the hunting coat off the hook near the gun cabinet. She would howl and run around like her tail was on fire. Her body would quiver because she was so excited about going hunting. My dad would even pump her up a little. Ask her if she wanted to go get some Chippies (squirrels) or dirty birds (pheasants). She howled so much that my mother would kick all three of us out the door.

We would load up the dog and make an inventory of what we had in the pockets of Dad's Old Coat. If we were going squirrel hunting...It was checking for the .22 shells for Dad and the .410 shells for me. It was a ritual. We had to have the squirrel call and two plastic bags for the squirrels

The same ritual was made during pheasant season. The plastic bags and the 20 gauge shells for the double barreled 20 gauge. We usually loaded one of the pockets with candy bars. Both of us are sweet toothed. Not to mention the dog.

The coat was also used for many duck and rabbit adventures. There was one thing that was always the same about each outing. It was that my mother would come out to bid us farewell before each venture into the outdoors. I can still remember her speech. She would tell me the same thing every time. "Guns are not toys. Treat your gun like it is always loaded. Always identify your target. When in doubt, do not shoot."

Mom had a different speech for dad. His speeches varied from season to season. It usually ended by my mother looking at my Dad's Old Coat and telling him that she was going to wash that NASTY thing when he came home. It was a joke between my dad and mom.

Mom knew that if she washed the coat it would take all of the magic and memories out of the pockets. She really didn't like the tattered blood stained thing that my father called a coat... but she knew that she should NEVER wash it.

Many adventures came and went during my childhood. I added a few stains to the pockets and I took over the ritual of checking the pockets as each season came and past. I kept the coat ready for the next outing.

I always pestered my dad about the coat. I told him I wanted one just like it. He would kid me and tell me that it was one of a kind and that he would give me the coat when I grew into it. I remember showing him a catalog with a coat that looked like his and telling him that the coat came in my size. He finally explained to me that he was NOT going to buy me a coat like his. He said that coats are grown into not purchased. He had been given that coat by his father and that I would be given the coat when I grew in size and hunting skills.

Years flew by. It was 1984. I had just gotten out of the Army. I went home to visit my mother. She picked me up at the airport. We talked all the way home. She told that my father would have been very proud of me if he were still around.

I stayed with my mother for the first few months after getting out of the army. Fall came and I had the itch to go hunting. I put my army coat on and took the 410 out of the gun cabinet. I filled the pockets with the proper tools. A squirrel call and two plastic bags were carefully placed in the pocket. I took a couple candy bars from the kitchen and was headed out the door.

My mother stopped me as I left. She said "Are you prepared for hunting?" I was little taken aback by the question. I told her: "Of course." She told me that I had forgotten a key part of my hunting adventure. We went back into the house. I was a little befuddled at what my mom was up to. She led me to the gun cabinet. She reached to the hook on the side of it and grabbed **IT**. She said **"It should fit now.** I am going to wash that NASTY thing when you get back." She smiled and sent me on my way.

ARE YOU AFRAID OF THE DARK?

It was the 20th of December 2008. Wisconsin small stream trout season had been closed since September 30th. I had some time so I decided a scouting mission was in order. I like scouting during the closed season due to the weeds being down and it is much easier to walk along the streams because of it. I was scouting a very small stream in Southwestern Wisconsin. Almost all of the streams in the area dump in to the Kickapoo River. I was very close to where it went in so I decided it warranted a look.

The Kickapoo River was quite clear and I could see the structure at the confluence. There was a prominent step drop as the stream emptied in. I stored the information away for another day. It looked like "Big Trout" water.

Season opened like it always does on the first Saturday of March. I had so many different places to check out from winter scouting that I did not make it back to this promising water until late May.

My buddy Joe "Dirt" Chadwick and I fish a lot together. I had him in tow this day and he is in really good shape so a jaunt through the tall weeds to the promising water was a fifteen-minute walk. We usually take turns on holes. It was Joe's turn to hit this hole first.

Joe's second offering was taken by a 16ish inch brown. Joe and I jaw at one another a lot when we fish. It is friendly banter. He was talking smack and looking at me while he battled the trout. All of a sudden the water next to his trout erupted and his trout was pushed sideways about 14 inches. Joe saw from my stare and expression that something odd was going on in the water. Joe adjusted his view to the trout on his line. The intruder was gone and Joe saw nothing. The trout was still flailing away and Joe continued his landing of the trout. We have an unwritten rule that when one of us has a trout on that needs netting, the other takes care of it without needing to be told to do it.

I waded in to the Kickapoo a little ways. I decided it was not a good day to go swimming. That step drop was directly in front of me. Joe started up his banter again. He said: "Old man get your fanny in there and net that fish." "What spooked you earlier?" I reached for my net and started to reach out to net the trout. I told Joe I believe a big northern has tried to eat your trout on the line. The trout was not ready to be netted and made another run. It tired out and Joe had it on its side coming in. The trout was about fifteen feet from my net and the water exploded again.

We both saw the intruder this time. It was about a 32-inch female brown. The dominant trout in the hole was pushing the 16 incher sideways. This trout was the deepest small stream trout I have ever seen. I guessed it at 10-13 pounds. The attack ceased as quickly as it began. We tried to entice another hit but it was fruitless.

June came and went. We walked out to that hole a minimum of fifteen times in June and never caught another trout. We varied our times of fishing and methods and still no hook ups. We decided to give the hole a two week rest and to have at it again. The weather was really hot and the main branch of the Kickapoo River's water temperatures were up. We did not want to land any trout and have them die due to lack of oxygen in the water because of the heat wave we had been having.

We met up at the 4th of July fireworks. We read each other's minds. We were on for the 5th of July. The weather had changed and the air and water temperatures were in a reasonable range now. After a short give and take conversation, it was decided I would have first crack at the big female. Joe had caught an absolute monster last July and it was my turn to try for a monster.

I called Joe at three a.m. that morning to make sure he was out of bed. He was not out of bed so I gave him a hard time and told to get in gear and meet me. I told him to wear drab colors and to give us every chance of catching the monster. Joe got there at four a.m. He was dressed in his pajama bottoms. They were brown plaid. He had some odd looking "hoody" jacket on. He didn't even have waders on. He had white low top tennis shoes on. I asked him if he was in some new type of "Urban Angler" attire. He said he could get wet if it was needed. He told me that the big female had left and we weren't going to catch it anyway.

Fishing in the dark is not my favorite outing. When trout get really large they turn in to nocturnal feeders. Every step in the pitch dark seems labored. Even flat ground becomes treacherous. It seemed like it took forever to get out there. We made it in thirteen minutes and I was in place and casting. It was 4:13 a.m. and I could not even see the end of my rod. We had picked this morning because of the imminent full moon. There was a full moon but the fog was really thick and it covered the moon. We hoped that the moon would help us see and full moons usually mean primary feeding periods. It was really eerie being out there in the dark. It made me question why we had gotten up so early.

At 4:43 am I had exhausted every option I had planned to use. The tall weeds had made the casting experience less than enjoyable on the edge of the darkness and one step from treading water in the main branch of the Kickapoo River. The weeds were a little more tolerable now due to me grooming the area for a half an hour while casting and the fourteen other trips to this area so far this summer. I told Joe he could "bat clean up." We looked in my box and there was one big fly in there that was not wet. It was a dumbbell eyed size 2 black bunny leech with red in the collar. He told me to stand back and watch the "Urban Angler" work his magic.

The bunny was quite heavy so he decided to make a two-part cast at it. He got it out part of the way and then kind of rolled it out there like spey casting.

Joe was able to get about five feet more distance on his cast than I had been doing. He ripped the leech through the area with long fast strips. The next thing we knew his pole was bent in half and the fish was screaming upstream in the Kickapoo River. All we could do was listen to the battle sounds.

It did a couple jumps and we heard the splashes when it came back to earth. We could not see due to the dark and fog. We were talking as he battled it. I told him big browns don't usually jump like that. They hunker down and do power runs. This one was doing power runs and trying to touch the sky. We both thought he had a northern on. We made sure we had the correct tool for the job before we came. There was a fresh 2X leader on. The Kickapoo is quite wide in the main channel. Luckily there were no down trees in the water. The battle took forever.

The battle in the fog was surreal. The line lurched different directions and at times strained and looked like it wanted to explode. Every time Joe gained a little line on the fish, it ran off another length of line into the darkness. I kept repeating to Joe: "Keep pressure on it. You have a new leader on and it is holding." Finally the trout tired and came towards us. The darkness and fog parted and the defeated leviathan came to my net. It was not a northern. It was not the female brown we had seen a month before. It was a gigantic hook jawed male brown. We both were giddy with the feeling of a battle won. The dark and the fog seemed much more tolerable as we stood there and smiled at each other. God, I love trout fishing. There is nothing better. The mammoth female will have to wait for another day.

ACT LIKE YOU HAVE BEEN THERE BEFORE

He rolled up in a big silver suburban. Bob Skoronski, retired Green Bay, Packer was driving. I fish pretty often with Bob Skoronski. This was the fifth time I had been trout fishing with Coach Bob Knight (retired). Coach Knight flashed me a big smile and we decided to gear up right there in the parking lot of the gas station where we usually met up. As the Coach geared up, I gave Coach something that I had been saving for him. It was a Curt Gowdy Parametric Fiberglass Rod. The rod was made by Berkley and was about 37 years old and in mint condition. It was a Curt Gowdy Signature Series. The Coach was honored by the gift. He got a little choked up. He said: "I have another friend that bought an original Ted Williams fly reel for me. Ted and I were good friends. I am going to put that reel on this rod and display it proudly in my den." During our last outing in 2007 I heard the Coach tell a

69

story about his old friend Curt Gowdy. Coach and Curt were good buddies and fished a lot together in the old days. When the two would go on fishing outings Curt would always buy a newspaper. During the long trips to the streams Coach would drive and Curt would go to the sports section and read the entire sports section en route to the stream. It was an up close and personal **Cavalcade of Sports** from Curt Gowdy to his good friend Coach Bob Knight. Coach said Curt's voice was so unique and it was an honor to ride with Curt to the streams. Coach said: "It was almost as good as the fishing."

Coach Knight had told me from other outings that he was a quantity guy not a quality guy. He liked lots of fish and was not a "big trout guy". We decided to target some spring creeks in Southwestern Wisconsin. I had quite a few of my friends tie up lots of flies for the Coach to use. The flies varied from nymphs to big ugly bunny leeches. Rich Femling, the owner of Rose-Creek Net Releases and Fly Boxes, gave me a fly box full of Bass Flies when we fished last to give to the Coach. Coach's eyes light up like a kid at Christmas as he perused the fly box.

The Coach already had his favorite fly tied on. It was a size eight girdle bug. I had a hard time getting him to change flies. He said it was "tried and true" and he had caught trout from Russia to Bozeman on the fly. I did get him to switch flies a couple times. Not long after the switch I would see him tying his "tried and true" back on.

On the first stretch of water I asked Coach Knight about getting back into coaching. Coach said he was done coaching. He did have some serious interest in the Georgia job when it opened but it never got past that. He said that his schedule is quite full nowadays with hunting and fishing. *ESPN* also takes a toll on his fishing already.

Coach and Bob Skoronski told stories of the old days when Skoronski use to drive all over the western United States to bird hunt with the Coach. Lots of times when I fish with Bob Skoronski he talks about his glory days with the Packers. This also came up during this outing. Coach caught a decent brown trout and I whipped out my camera and jokingly said, "Smile" to the Coach. Coach immediately frowned. I took the photo anyway. Knight looked at Skoronski and said: "Bob, haven't you taught Len what Lombardi instilled into your players?" I looked puzzled and the Coach elaborated. Lombardi used to say "Act like you have been there before." When his guys scored, they didn't do any outlandish dances or posing. "I don't smile in trout glory shots. I act like I have been there before." Both the Bobs smiled and we kept fishing.

It never fails that when the Bobs are together the Ice Bowl always comes up. Coach likes to hear what Bart Starr said in the huddle to his linemen before the "famous" quarterback sneak. Each time we have gone out it comes up. It is 30 degrees below zero and the Packers are on the one yard line and Starr turns to each of his linemen in the huddle and asks if they can go their way with a run. Starr turned to the right side and both of the offensive linemen said that Jethro Pugh was tired and they could go there. Pugh was a man mountain for those days and dwarfed almost all offensive linemen that he played against. They had scouted Pugh and when he got tired he stood higher in his four point stance.

The call in the huddle was fullback dive between right

guard and tackle. Starr lined up his troops and at the last second he decided to do a quarterback sneak due to the frigid conditions and Starr thought a hand off might be risky. Starr had a silent hand signal with his center that meant quarterback sneak. It depended on what butt cheek Starr goosed his center on which direction the sneak was going. The rest is history.

We wandered throughout the Driftless Area for the entire day. The Coach loves the small streams and solitude fly fishing brings. Many times I would go ahead of the Coach and leave him alone on the stream. I figured he has a hectic life and is surrounded by many people and trout fishing is a cleansing process. It is time to listen to the birds and watch the wind in the trees. Alone time... is very important.

At the end of the day Coach had landed 27 trout. There was a mixture of brooks and browns. All trout were caught on the "tried and true" girdle bug. A couple of glory shots were taken without a smile. I understood what he meant by the end of the outing. Coach shook my hand firmly as he left and flashed me a big smile. He said: "Thanks for the great day and it really looks like *You Have Been There Before.*"

THE GIFT

He went to the big trout stream in the sky November 1967. He left behind a 39 year old bride and 6 children. They varied in age from 17 to 3 years old. This was not how Len Harris Sr. had pictured his life ending. He had always believed that he would live to be an old grandpa with many grandchildren. He could not even envision his bride being left alone again. Fate could not be that cruel twice in her lifetime.

My mother (Jane) was actually quite familiar with death and being left alone. At age sixteen my mother was orphaned along with her three other siblings. My mother's parents each died of illness within a couple weeks of each other. The Chestelson children were thrown to the wind after their parents died. The youngest Kurt was sent away to northern Wisconsin to an Aunt that needed a young male to help with the farm (Wittenberg). My oldest uncle (Sig) was away in WWII. The oldest daughter (Betty Ann) went out on her own and landed in LaCrosse where she lived the majority of her life. My mother (Mary Jane) lived with the local Drug Store owners (Ackermann's) until she was 18. The Ackermann's were the family's closest friends and my mother did not have to move out of Gays Mills.

After my father died, my mother became Father and Mother to me. She stressed going to church weekly and it ended up that I went about five times a week from age 5 to 15. I was an altar boy. She set by example going to church at least that many times a week. Mom stressed that women should be treated differently than men and women should be cherished. My mother NEVER remarried or even thought about it. It would have been much easier on her with six children to have a husband... BUT... no one was taking my Dad's place.

My mother had her hands full with five daughters. My sisters ranged from toddler to High School Senior. She steered the Harris ship quite well and ALL of her children turned out as successful adults. I remember her stressing the need to manage one's finances and she instilled her work ethic in me. I spent many days in the ditches near the local high school picking up pop bottles for their two cent redemption. The nights in the rain with the flash light in my mouth and me crawling around on my hands and knees picking up night crawlers to sell to the local Sporting Goods store (three cents each) taught me well.

My father had given me the gift of loving the outdoors. My mother cultivated it. She made sure I had lures and decent fishing poles. She would go without so we kids were in decent clothing and were properly raised. She would drive me out in the country and drop me off stream side and pick me up just before dark so I could explore new trout streams.

I can remember being jealous of the kids with Dads and the toys the children got at Christmas and birthdays. My gifts were quite modest compared to the mini bikes and snowmobiles my friends received. As a child I did not understand it well. I didn't see when I was a kid that she was doing well to just put food on table and clothing on our backs.

I can remember breaking five pairs of glasses my sophomore year due to trying to play basketball. She always seemed to find money to get me a new pair. She was on the side lines for every game from freshman through senior year watching me play football. She was always terrified that I would get hurt. I was 6'3" tall and 162 as a senior. A "Bean Pole" as my sisters called me. My favorite sport in High School was track. My father had wanted me to be in track so Mom followed up on it and made sure I was there and she was there at every finish line cheering me on.

As an adult I have looked back many times and seen how truly good of a job my mother did raising me. She led by example when it came to work ethic. She juggled a couple jobs and was a full time mother and father to us six kids. I missed exactly two days of school from first grade through graduation. Both of those days were for funerals.

Mom gave me a ride to the airport when I left to go in

the army. She told me how proud she was of me and that I really looked good in my uniform. Germany was very far away and she wanted to make sure I wrote her weekly and called ever so often. I sent home $250.00 monthly to her while I was in the army to help her make ends meet. The only two times I have ever seen my mom cry was at my dad's funeral and when she sent me off at the airport.

I am retired now and have a fourteen year old daughter that worships her grandma and showers her with kisses and affection every time she is near. Anna tells grandma "thanks" often for being such a good mom to her dad. Mom has so many grandchildren and great grand children visiting she is never lonesome.

Just recently my mother had an 83rd birthday. We were talking and I told her about my thoughts as a child. She knew I felt that way and tried her hardest to provide for us. She told me she could see the disappointment in my eyes at Christmas when I got socks and underwear. Mom told me that my father gave me the best "Gift" of all... The Love of the Outdoors... I hated to disagree with her on her 83rd birthday, but I did.

I told her the greatest gift I had ever received was having **"HER"** as my mother.

THE ROAD TAKEN

The motley crew of kids from "the block" are all alive except for two. As children this crew hung out together. We all lived within three blocks of the Congregational Church in Gays Mills. I can remember many nights playing kick the can and tag and finally just after dark I would hear my mom. She would stand out on the porch and yell. "Bugs... come home..." Just one time and that was all that was needed and the gathering would disperse. Most times I was with my cousin Chris. He usually went home with me.

Chris was a year older than me but he was socially many years older than me. We hung out together every summer and he usually ate at my house every lunch and dinner. I can remember lots of crazy things we did together. Once we found some old condoms in a drawer at my house. I believe I was thirteen. I didn't know what they were. I am pretty sure Chris did. He had me blow them up and put them on a string and walk on Main Street with them. He told me they were balloons. As I think back... He didn't carry a balloon that day on a string up and down Main Street. He made an excuse why he had to go home. He really didn't. He watched from a distance as I paraded up and down Main Street with my balloons.

As we got older, Chris developed lots faster than me. He had muscles and street savvy to go with them. He protected me and actually beat up anyone who messed with me. I can remember him beating up a kid from Seneca that was a whole head taller than him because the kid shoved me to the ground. Chris was the brother I never had.

As we grew older, we got in a couple scrapes that my mother was angry at me for not showing more common sense. In middle school Chris and I hung out together also. Chris was six feet tall as an eighth grader and was much bigger than me. He outweighed me by 30 pounds. He defended me quite a few times and got a reputation for being a good fighter.

Chris told me what sex was and I didn't believe him. I thought it was impossible and he had to be lying. I asked my mom and she was flabbergasted that I had learned about it from Chris. I can remember her saying once. "He is a little too educated."

My mom didn't like the direction my life was taking. She thought I was getting in too much trouble and fights along with Chris. She kept me closer to home for a while. Chris and I still hung out but not so much. Chris worked with his dad as a plumber's assistant almost every summer and was an accomplished apprentice at age fourteen. I hung out a little on job sites. I had no mechanical inclinations and was actually a little afraid of tools. I had never been taught how to use them due to my father going to heaven when I was ten.

Chris and I grew apart because of him working with his dad and he found a new social group to hang with. My Mother forbid me to go with the group. She said they were trouble.

Chris befriended one of the guys he got in a fight with. The guy's name was Mitch. Chris and Mitch did everything together. I was left in the dust because of being timid and was socially inept. I didn't fit in with the crowd he hung with anymore. Chris and Mitch went off on a different road. They hung with the older crowd and were very gullible. They were often talked into doing things that skirted normal rules.

It was fall and Chris went out for football as a freshman. He made the team and actually was getting playing time at practice. I use to watch him at practice and was jealous. I was 5'7" and 100 pounds as a ninth grader. Not a football player and NOT tough like my cousin Chris.

It was Apple Festival weekend and lots of us kids were on Main Street enjoying the festivities. The Sheriff's Department screamed by and an ambulance shortly thereafter. The gossip on the street was that two young guys were squirrel hunting and a grouse had flown up and one of the guys had shot his hunting partner at point blank range with a shotgun and one of the kids was dead.

Four days later I was a pall bearer for my Cousin Chris. Chris had been killed by his buddy Mitch. He had died instantly from a shotgun blast to his head and neck. There was controversy about this accident that went on for years later.

The years churned by slowly. My uncle needed a new plumber's helper. I took Chris' place. I didn't know which end of the tool to use. The only thing I ran ok was a shovel. My mechanical skills were nonexistent. High School flew by. I went to technical school for Heating and Refrigeration servicing. I barely passed due to being afraid of electricity and tool stupid. I was to graduate and become a plumber and furnace technician for my uncle. I was to replace Chris.

I was all thumbs and quickly figured out that it was not my calling. My road was steered for me for a while and I finally got on path again. I went in to the Army at age 20 and steered my own ship and took my own roads from then on.

Seven years, one month and eleven days in the Army taught me how to be on my own two feet and I grew from a child to a man. Five of those years were in Germany. I learned to love German cooking and German beer. I left behind an ex-wife in Germany.

Today my life looks much different. I am married to a wonderful woman and it was our anniversary is on June 3rd. We have been married 21 years. We have a beautiful daughter. I sometimes wonder where my path would have led me if the DETOURS had not happened.

MEMORIES ARE FOREVER...

Dad left Wednesday night. He drove up to his brother's to deer hunt. I watched him leave. It was almost painful watching his yellow van pull out of the driveway. I wanted to go so badly. I was old enough to do ALL of the other hunting and fishing things with him. But "NOT" rifle deer hunt.

The phone rang and we were all sitting around the television watching the Packers play the Lions on Turkey Day. I flew to the phone. It was my dad. He told me he would be home late that evening. I asked him how he did. He told me a doe and a big buck. Mom took the phone and told Dad that I was driving her crazy talking about deer hunting. She hung up and said to the family that dad would be home late that evening.

I asked my mom if I could put my new deer hunting coat on and wait for my dad outside. The coat was still in the box. It was a wool black and red plaid deer hunting coat. She told me not to put it on right away. So I waited about two minutes and put it on. I took my five-gallon bucket and went out to the end of the driveway. After about three hours my mother called out to me and told me to come inside.

I was really mad. I wanted to show my mother I WASN'T too little to deer hunt. I wanted her to tell Dad that I had sat on that bucket for hours completely still. "Just like a good buck hunter." I always listened to my mom. I went to the porch with my bucket.

It wasn't much longer and dad rolled into the drive. I sprinted to the end of the driveway. My dad had a huge smile when he saw me. I was in my miniature deer hunting coat. He had not seen it before then. Mom told him she bought it for me as an early Christmas present.

We all helped my dad take the deer off the roof. I heard my mom and dad talking. Dad asked mom why she bought that coat for me. Mom said I was so disappointed that I couldn't go. She had to do something to ease my pain. Dad said "That will only fan his flames. He is still too young to go."

I made my dad tell me the complete story of both deer he had gotten. Complete with the way the winds were coming from and the weather. I wanted to know even the littlest details so I could feel like I was there.

Sunday morning came and Dad and I got up early and went to the Gas Station to swap lies with all the other hunters. I wore my new deer hunter's coat. All the locals were there. Each hunter shared their hunting stories. It was my dad's turn to tell his story. Dad started out the story slowly. He hesitated between sentences and I couldn't help it. I finished his sentence for him. ALL the locals roared in laughter. They knew I had not gone along and I knew the story by heart in only four days.

The harsh winter came to visit and seemed to last forever. My dad and I spent time on the Mississippi ice fishing to pass the cold Wisconsin months. I really liked being alone with him. It was one on one time with my dad. I did not have to share him with my sisters.

Spring came and this meant many different outdoor activities with my dad. Just him and I. Bird hunting and fishing were the norm every weekend. The winds became cold and my dad was getting the deer hunting itch again. I was angry. I knew there was ONLY one more year...one more year of waiting at the end of the driveway for my dad.

My dad loaded up the van again and left at dusk on Wednesday night. As my dad left, he rolled down the window of the van; he said, "Next year you will be going along with me." My mom waved bye to my dad and told me NO waiting in the driveway this year. I could wait on the porch.

Thursday came and no call from Dad. I went out onto the porch to sit. I decided to raise all of my dad's deer horns up to the top of the porch. I left the row of nails below his horns. That row was going to be where ALL my horns were going to hang.

Friday came and again no call. I went back out to the porch. I organized all the ice fishing gear. Put new line on the jig poles and took all the mono out of the eyes of the jigs in the jig boxes. Saturday night I organized my shelves on the porch. I liked most of all my firsts with my dad. There were tail feathers of the first three ducks I shot and my first pheasant's tail feather. Then there was my favorite. It was my grouse tail. Those dang things were so hard to hit. The rest of the things I organized were two squirrel tails and a red and white daredevil and my *Mepps* spinner from my first trout. Each had special memories from Dad and me.

Sunday night I saw light at the end of the driveway. I grabbed my deer hunting coat and went out to meet my dad. I was my dad's yellow van. I went to the driver's door. It wasn't my dad driving. It was my uncle Dudley. I asked where my dad was. He didn't speak. He got out of the van and went into the house. My mother and uncle walked into another room and closed the door. I t seemed like they were in there forever. There was a knock on the door.

It was my two uncles. They were my mother's brothers. They also went into the room with Uncle Dudley and mom. All the adults came out of the room and mom called us all to the kitchen table.

She had us all sit down. She started to cry. All my uncles consoled her. My Uncle Dudley told us that my dad was hunting with him and Dad got a big buck. Later that evening my father died of an apparent heart attack at Grandmother's house.

Mothers and fathers please take your children outdoors. Show them the wonders of nature. Get them out from in front of the television and video games... *Please?*

BOWER

One of my buddies from my old job contacted me. Eric (old buddy) told me that he belonged to a Midwest hunting website. One of the sons of a member was being shipped out to Iraq. The website was having a going away party for Aaron Bower. He wanted me to come. I had something planned so I didn't go. Eric emailed me and said the party was a great send-off to a real American Hero. I felt for Aaron because I was in the Army for 7 years and almost ended up in Iran when the embassy was taken over in 1970s.

I saw some of the photos of his send off on the hunting website. Aaron in his uniform was quite impressive. My days in the service came back to me. I remember the feelings I had of pride in country. I smiled at the photos and decided I was happy I wasn't the one going to Iraq.

Couple years went by. Eric contacted me again. He said that Aaron had gone to Iraq and was injured. The hunting website was having a benefit for him. Eric wanted to know if I would donate a trip to a fallen veteran. I have donated numerous Trout Fishing Trips to trout Unlimited Chapters and a few Cancer Drives. It was a NO BRAINER. Eric said it would be raffled off and the proceeds would be given to Aaron for unpaid medical expenses I didn't even ask what Aaron's injuries were. I said YES immediately.

Eric told me he would contact me and tell me who had won the Fishing Trip with me at the raffle. The raffle was held late September. I received notice from Eric in October that the raffle was a HUGE success and my trip was raffled off for 3,000 dollars. A local VFW post in Iowa was the winner of the raffle. The 3,000 dollars was given to Aaron's dad who was guardian nowadays. Aaron was unable to make his own decisions because of the severe injuries he sustained in Iraq. The VFW commander said that after the raffle the entire VFW membership had voted and they voted to give the trip to the Fallen Veteran and his dad. Phil was Aaron's dad's name.

Phil called me right away. He wanted to go trout fishing with Aaron immediately. I told Phil that Wisconsin's season had closed September 30th. I could tell from Phil's voice he was quite disappointed. We talked throughout the winter. Phil was as excited as Aaron to go trout fishing. A couple times during the phone calls from Phil I asked questions about Aaron. Phil was very vague. I asked Phil to talk to his son (Aaron). Phil always had a reason for me NOT talking to his son. Aaron had one infection or another or was going to therapy or just wasn't up for talking.

I sent Phil and Aaron many photos through the winter of previous trout fishing outings. Phil always told me he passed on the stories and photos to Aaron. I never did get to talk to Aaron in person. We must have shared 40 emails and 20 phone conversations through the winter.

As the date grew closer I needed to know what Aaron's physical limitations were. I needed to plan a good outing for Aaron and his dad. Both anglers were worm anglers and had fished Iowa exclusively. They had never fished Wisconsin before. I finally got Phil to tell me a little about the injuries. Phil was vague and told me that Aaron was in Iraq on the battlefield and his company was attacked in the middle of the night. Phil said "Aaron was injured very badly." I tried to get more out of him but Phil was kind of selective with his information.

I was to meet Phil and Aaron at the park in my hometown. Phil said they were accomplished campers and he and Aaron had camped many times in the past. It was raining buckets the day before and I called Phil and tried to re-schedule. I wanted Aaron to have a quality outing. Phil said absolutely NOT. We were fishing no matter what. He said he didn't care if they caught anything. The father and son NEEDED this outing and they had talked about it all winter. I said okay, I would meet them at first light.

I rolled up to the park and it was still raining buckets. Phil told me they would camp on the far north side of the campgrounds near the river. I found the site right away. The Iowa license plate was a good indicator and there were NO other campers in the park. I had checked some of the streams on the way to see their clarity. They were iffy. Phil met me at my truck. He had huge smile and said come meet Aaron. I went in to the tent and met Aaron... He was sitting in the dark tent and nodded his head a lot. The rain was still coming down hard. He didn't talk much. Phil did most of the talking. I learned that both of the trout anglers were kind of new to trout fishing and they had fished for bass, carp, bullheads and panfish in Iowa and were QUITE good at it. This was the way Phil described it. I told them that because of their Iowa plates it would be better if they rode with me. Lots of locals didn't like out of state anglers. Phil said okay.

I had both of the anglers change into their gear at the campgrounds. I decided that changing in a dry tent would be better than changing in a downpour. I had dressed in my waders and gear at home. Both anglers put on hip boots and rain coats. Dad tore down the campsite and we piled into my truck with all OUR gear. It was still dark out and we drove to the stream.

We parked near the stream. It was not light enough to fish. I thought I should get some more information from the dad and son on their fishing limitations. Dad said: " Aaron and I fished five days a week before he went to the gulf." Aaron and he were skilled anglers before his accident. Dad told me since the accident Aaron's balance was poor and his endurance wasn't there anymore. Dad also told me that Aaron's confidence was lacking since his injury and it was really important to HIM that his son had a good time.

Finally the rain stopped and the sun came out. We fished for two hours. Aaron caught ten trout and his dad caught two. Aaron tired out quickly and dad said it was time to go home. We walked back to my truck. Aaron had been quiet most of the outing. Aaron spoke up on the way back to Dad's truck. He told me he had a wonderful time and hoped we could do it again. I could see his Dad in the backseat of my truck in my rear view mirror. Dad had such a HUGE smile I thought his face might break. I sent both of them on their way and thought that this was one of my favorite trips.

Aaron's company was attacked at night. The company had dug foxholes near the Tanks and Armored Personnel Carriers. The armored vehicles would give them added protection from enemy attacks. Aaron was in his foxhole defending his position and one of Aaron's company's tanks decided to change locations for tactical reasons. The tank ran over Aaron's foxhole and crushed Aaron's skull while doing so.

Aaron had nothing bad to say about the military during our fishing trip. He was NOT angry about what happened.

Aarron Bower is "A True American Hero."

THE LITTLE THINGS

My buddy Bob is 74 years old. Bob and I have fished together for about fifteen years. On almost every outing he talks about his neighbor. Bob talks about the "Old Timer" that lives right next to him. I usually crack a smile when Bob calls someone an old timer. How old must someone be.... to be called an old timer by a 74 year old guy? I asked Bob this exact question. Bob told me that he has lived by the same family for 40 years. His neighbor and he have swapped fishing stories for the entire time.

During my fifteen years of fishing with Bob I had heard many stories of his old timer neighbor. The stories seemed magical. Bob had a neighbor story to share each time we fished. For a couple years I thought that Bob's neighbor was a character in a book that Bob read and shared a chapter with me each time we fished. Bob reassured me that his neighbor was real and that someday I would have the privilege to fish with him. The stories were all trout or salmon related. They varied from the Brule for steelhead to the Upper Peninsula for tiny brook trout.

About six years ago the "old timer" stories weren't part of our fishing outing. I waited the entire trip for Bob to tell me one of the magical stories. Bob told me that his neighbor was really busy nowadays and didn't have time to share his tales from the past. The neighbor's wife had developed Alzheimer's disease and he was taking care of her at home. She was "not" going to a nursing home.

Two weeks ago Bob and I fished. At the beginning of our outing Bob told me that I was finally going get to meet his elderly neighbor. I was looking forward to meeting this Patriarch of the fishing world. I would get to put a face with the many tales I had heard about in the last 15 years. Bob said that his neighbor finally had time to go fishing with us. His bride of 66 years had passed away two weeks prior. He had taken care of her by himself for the last six years at home.

Bob rolled up in his big silver suburban. The passenger door came open and Don slowly exited the vehicle. Bob introduces me to "Donnie" ...This is what Bob called him. I decided I would call him Don to show respect. He stands about five feet, six inches. Father Time has caused him to actually stand about five foot, three. He has osteoporosis and he has a humped over posture. There are small tufts of white hair on each temple. . He told me that he lost most of his hair in his early 40s. He chuckled and said he had lost most of his hair before I was born. He has the classic frame round gold wire rim spectacles. They sit on the end of his nose and he looks over them more than through them. His face is road map of many years of smiling. His forehead is engraved with deep furrows from the long journey of life.

At the beginning of our fishing adventure Don asked me "not" to take any photos of him, so my description of him will have to suffice. We all got back in the vehicle and we were on our way to the "Best" brook trout stream I knew.

We got out and geared up. I told Don we were going after brookies. He asked if there were any obvious hatches lately and told him no. He smiled and said: "Good, I can hardly see those little flies anymore, let alone tie one on." Don took out his 5 weight and strung it up. I watched him struggle when gearing up. His vision was quite poor and he looked over his glasses the entire time. Don finally allowed me to set-up his rod. I put a size twelve bead headed Biot Bug on for him and blaze orange strike indicator about four feet up. Don asked me what that the orange thing was. I told him a strike indicator. He had me take it off and put a dry on instead as an indicator. It only took five minutes to walk across the open pasture and get Don on the water. Don's casting abilities were still there and he had a couple hits quite quickly. He missed the hits. Don told me he didn't even see the hits. I started alerting him to bites by saying "Bite...bite..." After about two more misses, Don asked for the blaze orange strike indicator to be put back on.

Don said: " I haven't fished for at least seven years. It is amazing how much you can really miss *The Little Things* in life. Bob and I had decided that a short outing was the best idea for an old timer. On the way home Don told me that he had an excellent time and when we went again that he preferred if I would call him "Donnie". I told him absolutely. Donnie said all of his friends called him Donnie and that he really wasn't that old...

A Blade Of Timothy Grass

The weather was not the best. It was windy and even spitting snow. Both anglers took long rods with stiff backbones to battle the wind. We went in at a bridge on permissioned property. The father and son combination of Tim and Matt Noll, had clearly fished together numerous times. The father Tim let the son have the first hole. Tim watched closely as Matt presented a black woolly bugger with green crystal flash to the finicky trout. Three casts in the hole and Matt landed a decent driftless brown. Matt still showed every fish he caught to his Dad. It was a childhood thing that had continued over to adulthood. Tim always beamed with approval and flashed a huge smile back at Matt. I notice Tim did the same thing each time he caught a fish. This Dad & Son team truly loved fishing together. They each shared tips and hints to one another on casting and placement of casts. It was a pleasure to watch such a well oiled machine.

We plodded on battling the wind. It was Dad's turn to fish the next hole. There was a buddy system going on. They had an unwritten rule for years. They alternated holes. Dad placed himself on a beautiful hole. The hole was quite a puzzle with multiple currents and eddies. Tim and Matt discussed how best to attack the hole. They decided that the hole looked like it could hold a really big trout and the hole should be attacked to attempt catching the Big Boy of the hole first. They conferenced and decided the trout would be at the step drop at the top of the hole tight right. Tim placed himself for the cast accordingly. The cast was well planned and executed. Tim did manage a hook-up of a large trout that put quite a BEND on the long fast action graphite rod. The big trout did not cooperate.

We decided to move upstream and try another enormous hole. Matt was still using the long fast action graphite due to the wind and the long holes we had been fishing. Matt was throwing a cone headed turkey leech. Father Noll was throwing a weighted hornberg on the same type of long fast action rod. We had a couple hookups with none landed in the deep enormous hole. Matt managed a LARGE chub.

The wind was not our friend this morning.

We went to lunch and talked plans for the afternoon. Father and Son told me that they wanted to catch some brookies. Off we went to the Brookie Lair. The brookie stream I picked was deep and lined with many willows tight up to the edge of the water.

Father and Son exited the truck. We stood at the rear of the truck for a while discussing strategy on what we should use. There were lots of willows to contend with here. Both were confident in their casting abilities. Father Noll took out a fast action graphite 3 weight, 7 feet long.

Matt took out an old rod... He called it a *Wanigas*... I

said what the heck kinda rod is that? Matt said it was Saginaw written backwards. *Wanigas*... I have never heard of that kind of the rod until yesterday. Matt explained to me that the rods were built in a guy's garage for the first couple years of the company existence in Saginaw, Michigan. After the rod became popular, the guy and his buddy took the rod building out of the garage. The company was now closed for quite some time.

I looked at the very old fiberglass rod. It was OLD and showed considerable wear. One of the eyes was wrapped with a different aqua colored thread. The rod had certainly seen some miles on it. I chuckled to myself and thought that SOFT action old beater will have a hard time in here. The willows and the wind would have the younger angler frustrated quite quickly.

Matt and Tim conferred and the Wanigas was what Matt wanted to use here. Then Matt put an OLD reel on it.......that he said it had no DRAG and he would have to palm it if he got any big fish. Both anglers switched from hip books to chest waders.

Matt then asked his Dad: "Is this the right kind of grass?" Father Noll said: "Use a piece of Timothy Grass to secure the ferules." Matt picked a blade of Timothy Grass and his dad told how to put the rod together with the one blade of grass... just the right way to get the rod to fit together properly. This old clunker rod had seen so much use that the ferules were worn out and fitted loosely. The only way it would stay together was to put a shim (blade of grass) between the ferules. This stop seemed to start out wrong in my mind. I thought we would be going back to the truck soon for a functional rod.

Matt started with a pink squirrel and Father Noll started with a biot bug. The trout were having no part of what we were throwing. The old fiberglass rod was holding its own on the windy day. Matt and his dad put the same black crystal flash woolly bugger on... and they both put on an indicator. The indicator was a blaze orange Lindy's Rig walleye float. They fished the bugger like nymphs with slow strips and a pause in between.

The first cast Matt hooked up on a sweet brookie. That old soft action Wanigas had a huge bend in it. After a long battle with that soft 3 weight fiberglass rod, Matt landed the nice brookie. Matt beamed a huge smile at his Dad and Tim nodded and smiled.

Tim stepped up to bat. Tim with his newer fast action rod got quite a bit more distance on his casts than Matt. The distance did not prove fruitful. Tim couldn't buy a bite. Father and son were fishing the long beaver dam hole exactly the same. They compared their retrieve styles. Both were doing the same type of retrieve. The depths of the indicators were the same. Tim told Matt it was his hole again.

Matt was landing trout hand over fist. Father Noll watched in amazement. They switched again. I watched each angler closely to see if there was any difference in their retrieves or cast placements. The only thing I saw different was the distance Tim was casting. I told him to shorten up his casts. Maybe Tim was lining the trout and spooking them. Matt said it had to be the rod. I smirked and thought to myself, "Ya... Right... It was the rod."

I watched for a while again. Matt had caught five trout and his Dad had one bite with no hook-up. I suggested a rod change. Matt took the graphite and Father Noll took the Special Fiberglass rod... The one with the Timothy Grass holding it together. I joked that the old rod had some special MOJO... Father Noll started catching fish just like Matt.

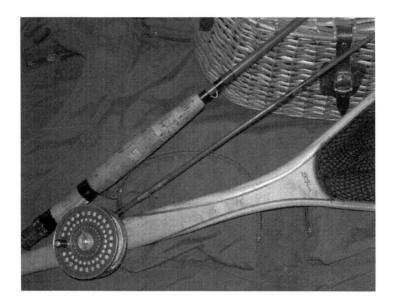

Tim sat down the fast action graphite rod and said he would pick it up on the walk back. The father & son team used the same rod. They just handed it off after each fish caught. We fished the beaver dam hard and fished upstream for about two hours. There was still fishing time left. I suggested another stream. The father and son said almost in unison. "No thank you." "We have caught more trout than we EVER have in an entire day. We are calling it quits." As we walked back downstream to pick up the other rod we talked and did a count of fish caught. That morning they caught two trout and a chub between them. That afternoon with the *Wanigas* they caught over 30 trout each.

The only thing I can figure out is...

Maybe the old Wanigas rod was MAGICAL. Maybe it was the Blade Of Timothy Grass... Maybe it was the aqua blue thread holding on the eye... Maybe the fish gods were smiling on an Old Rod... Or maybe... It was the magic of a father and son fishing together.

THE CURMUDGEON

Curmudgeon
definition:
cur·mud·geon
Function: noun
Etymology: origin unknown
1 : a crusty, ill-tempered, and usually old male trout
cur·mud·geon·li·ness /-lE-nes/ noun-
 cur·mud·geon·ly /-lE/ adjective

A typical life expectancy of a small stream trout varies. If a trout finds a good stream or "home" and it has the necessary cover and forage, a trout could live to an age of around twelve years.

Five years ago I found such a "home". I walked around the bend in a stream and it was before me. It is a *WOW* hole. A *WOW* hole is one that totally screams out "Large Trout Home".

The top of the hole has a current line for oxygen and feed source. The hole itself is an old farm field bridge that has caved in ages ago. The boulder at the base of the bridge causes a severe step drop in depth. A step drop is where the depth of a hole goes from two feet to eight feet deep in about two feet distance.

The rest of the hole has some cover on the left and a couple ambush points for The Curmudgeon to attack his prey. The hole is about eight feet deep in the center. This allows the trout to stay in this hole year round.

I scouted the hole from downstream in a crouched position for a short time. It was March and the vegetation was limited. I watched the water. I saw no obvious feeding action. This hole was so far off the main roadway it screamed Large Trout. It was way too far of a walk for the casual angler.

I thought for a long time how to attack this hole. The water was cold in March, so any possible large fish would be in the slow moving deep water. I needed to make a cast way up into the current to hide the splash of my cast.

I was worried that a smaller fish might spook the hole first and I would not have a chance at The Curmudgeon. I figured if I was going do it, it would be on the first five casts.

I casted for a hour at the hole with not even a whisper of a fish in the hole. From my experience, I learned that old male trout are very territorial. When they are really old they chase ALL other trout out of the hole. They are crusty and ill tempered.

After the hour I decided to walk out into the hole and carefully map the bottom for structure. The best way I knew was to actually wade the entire hole. I started at the edges and worked my way to the fast water funnel. The fast water funnel end was clearly over my waders so I poked my pole into the depths. Something flew out of the depths and did a circle in the hole and then stopped on the other far side of the hole. It was obviously a big fish due to the wake it created in the hole. I had thrown the kitchen sink at this fish and had not even gotten a bump.

I visited this hole annually for five years, about ten times each year. I varied my casts. I varied time of day and night. I even sat on the hole in the middle of the night. I caught NO trout.

Last fall I was talking to a friend about The Curmudgeon. He asked what I had tried so far. I told him all of the tricks I tried. He asked me if I had ever tried to anger the trout. Make it so angry it would hit out of anger. I had my friend tell me what he meant by that.

He said that an Old Trout that big would be territorial and if I casted in and ripped the presentation through the hole at 100 miles an hour. I might anger it enough into hitting. I had tried everything else...So what the heck. I looked in my box and saw the biggest and heaviest thing in my box and let her rip.

Second cast and I was bringing it as fast as I possibly could and it slammed it. It went deep and hunkered down on the bottom. After a change of direction battling it, I got it to the top of the water. I was not disappointed. It was well worth five years of hunting this fish.

I dubbed him *"The Curmudgeon"* and sent him on his way.

PG-13 Spider Bite

I learned an important lesson a few opening days ago. I had my gear all ready. The reels were clean and new line on all them. I checked my net for holes and cleaned all the old line out of the eyes of the hooks. I did all of my before opening day rituals. I took my waders out of the garage. They had been hanging there all winter. I always wash my gear at the end of the season so my stuff is ready to jump right in to opening morning of the coming year. Wading boots made wet and sitting by the chair by the door. I hardly slept a wink. The day before opener I am like a kid waiting for Christmas morning to come.

I was awake before the alarm. I had placed all my gear at the kitchen table the night before . Put my wool socks on and two pairs of long underwear. It gets pretty cold wading in ten degree temps in March here in Wisconsin. I put my waders on and laced up my wading boots. It is six a.m. and I am in my truck putting on my safety belt. I feel a little pain in my groin. I ignore it. Off I go to my favorite stream.

About ten minutes out of town and my groin is starting to throb and get really warm. I get out of the truck and drop two pairs of long underwear and waders. Under my two pairs of long johns is a dead spider in my fly area of my inner layer. I put it in a fly box right away.

A little closer examination revealed a emerging problem. I decided fishing is going to have to wait. I went straight home. I am allergic to most insect bites and bee stings. I gave a little extra gas because my problem is growing. The pedal is to the metal and my truck is pointed home. By the time I get home I am walking bow legged. I tear off my waders as I get in the house. Afraid I might have missed another spider.

I kick my wife out of bed. She is a Registered Nurse. I show her my problem. She stares in disbelief. The whole right side of my entire unit along with its accessories are about three times the regular size. Wife says a trip to the **Emergency Room** is in order. She gives me a ice pack to help with the swelling. Just before we leave my wife looks at me with a smile and asks if we can use it once before we go. I just roll my eyes at her and off we go to the ER. She responds "ONLY kidding."

The ER doctor is awakened from a evening nap. He is one of my fishin' buds. He examines the problem. The first thing he asks was if I had been sleeping around. My wife answers before I can. She says absolutely NOT. I had saved the spider and I show it to him. He takes the spider with him and I assume he is going to try to identify the beast. He tells me he has to go look up something and will be right back.

He returns with six other male staff members from the

hospital to see the THING. I get a little angry at him. He has a polaroid camera with him. He wants to take a photo of it. I ask him why he needs a photo? Is it for diagnosing it? He just laughs and says NO. I tell him no photos. The doctors had looked under the microscope and say the spider is not poisonous. One of the doctors says in parting; "We sure don't need a microscope to examine him." After eight epinephrine shots and a precautionary antibiotic shot and calming down, the doctor tells me I am hypersensitive to bug bites and stings. He determines this from my medical records through the years. I had many a run in with bees and spiders. I am ready to go fishing again. I remember purposely wading in deep water that day so the cold water could ease my pain.

The incident was not over that morning. It was a painful reminder for me for four weeks. The bite caused the skin to swell so much it split in a couple places. I hate spiders. The moral to this story is: **"Check your waders opening morning!!!!**

THE END OF AN ERA

Geno called me at home. He told me that he was giving his wood cook stove to his son, Steve. The wood cook stove was not a good auxiliary heat source anymore. He told me that Steve was bringing him a high efficiency wood stove to take its place. I had told Geno on an earlier visit that I wanted to get a photo of the *"Monarch"* Wood Cook Stove before he banished it to the garage at Steve's house.

Geno McManamy is his name. I always like talking with him. He reminds me of my father. Geno has forgotten more hunting and fishing memories than most people will experience in a lifetime. Geno is one of the last remaining members of the "Reber's Gas Station Gang". All of the members would meet at the only gas station in town on Sunday mornings. They would drop their wives off at church and then they would ALL meet up at the gas station and swap hunting and fishing lies. The noon whistle meant church was over and time to pick up the wives.

"Monarch" was one of the wood cook stoves of the *Malleable Iron Range Company*, Beaver Dam, Wisconsin. The company was in business from 1896 until 1985. This model was made around the turn of the century.

I drove to Gays Mills today to take a couple photos and get some history behind the stove. Geno and his wife Marilyn were at home. Marilyn told me that she learned how to cook on that wood cook stove from her mother Anna. Both of them were not sure if all the things Marlyn cooked on that old Monarch would taste the same on an electric stove. The smell of wood some how gave the food a more appealing taste.

Geno said: "It wasn't so much the taste but the memories that go along with the old *Monarch*." The wood stove signified days gone by. "Simpler days." We sat down at his kitchen table and talked about the old days. That cook stove prepared the first family meal for Geno and Marilyn when they were newlyweds. It warmed many baby bottles for their children.

Geno equated the old relic to hunting and fishing. "I cleaned many a trout and northern on that butcher block table next to the stove. Marylin would have the bacon grease at the perfect temperature by the time I was done cleaning my brookies. She popped them right in the grease. I can smell the aroma right now as we speak. I can taste the crisp tails of those mouth watering brookies."

"Many a deer was butchered on that butcher block table. The back straps were the first things to be fried on the cook stove. It usually happened the same night the deer was harvested. Lots of onions and green peppers were in the pan. My son and two daughters watching their mother cook. The whole family was living an experience that is seldom re-enacted nowadays. ALL of my children are good cooks."

Marilyn also told Geno she had baked a couple apples pies in the electric stove and that they tasted almost as good. She wasn't sure if her rhubarb pie would taste the same out of a electric stove. She would get back to him soon on that. The rhubarb was thawing in the sink.

Geno asked Marilyn if she could cook all the things he was used to on a new fangled electric range. Marilyn reassured Geno she could. Geno said: "Even squirrel and morels?" "Yes dear," she responded. They both were not certain that the house would be the same without the *Monarch*. It wasn't just the way the food smelled or tasted being cooked on that old stove... It was the memories that went with it.

The *Monarch* had been retired as the family cooking stove for over a decade ago. A new-fangled electric stove had replaced it. It was used as a wood heat stove nowadays. It was fired up on special occasions (Family Gathering) for sentimental reasons.

The stove is being taken out the last weekend of September. The memories will stay in that house. It truly is a shame that progress has made some of the good old days obsolete. Computers and game stations have supplanted the meetings around the table in the kitchen. The wood cook stove in the background making the food just right. Just the way you remember it. Then there were the talks about the day's happenings at the table. The stove was very much a symbol of the past. Geno said: "It ain't no microwave." Geno and Marilyn hold on tightly to their memories of the old days.

It was a simpler time when families spent more time talking and cooking, experiencing life together in front of that old *Monarch*.

Update: Since I wrote this story *Geno McManamy has become a resident of heaven. Geno was one the men who took me under his wing after my father died. He took me hunting and fishing and taught me many things about the outdoors. Geno, we all miss you and hope there is a wood stove in heaven to prepare the food perfectly like Marilyn does.*

GONE FISHIN'

I drove to the nursing home to pick up my wife in blowing snow. She had worked a double shift because of the bad weather here in Wisconsin. The nurse that was to work the shift could not make it in because of blowing snow. Barb left her little car in the parking lot. I barreled through the snow with my SUV. I parked between the snowdrifts and went inside to look for my wife. When I didn't see her at the nurse's station, I walked around to find her.

A white-haired gentleman in a wheel chair asked me if I was lost. The 80-ish year old man introduced himself as "Trout". I asked the guy if that was his real first name. "Trout" said that his real name was something else but he has been known as "Trout" since his childhood.

I smiled politely at Trout, and noticed that my wife

was nowhere to be found just yet. Trout looked at me with a twinkle in his eye and asked, "You want to see a real trout?" He gestured for me to follow him through his door.

There were two names on the door. One of them said: "Trout Swenson." There were two beds in the room. It was quite obvious which side Trout lived in. The right side of the nursing home room was like a shrine to trout.

There were photos plastered all over the wall and four huge trout mounts on the wall. The mounts were old and awe inspiring. Three of the mounts were male trout and all of them were over 30 inches. Each trout was mounted on a gnarly piece of driftwood. The alligator teeth on each trout were fearsome looking. The final trout on the wall was at least 36 inches. It was the deepest female trout I had ever seen. I guessed the trout's weight at between 16 and 18 pounds. The wall also was adorned with three fishing rods. And there was a HUGE net mounted directly over his head.

I told Trout I was a husband of one of his nurses. He said, "You must be Spinner." I smiled at Trout and nodded my head. He smiled and said, "Sit on down." Our conversation quickly turned to trout fishing. Trout had been born and raised in Richland County. He has fished the local streams his whole life. He told me his "temporary" stay at the nursing home was putting a cramp on his fishing outings. Trout had injured his hip on the stream last fall.

I asked him about the four trout mounts on the wall. I asked him the lengths and weights. He started out the descriptions with the same opening line. *"If my memory serves me right I caught that trout on a night crawler on my fly rod."*

The four mounts varied from 32 inches to 36 inches in length. He said he never weighed any of his trout, he only measured them. All of his small stream trout fishing was done locally. All of the trout on the wall were caught in a 100 mile radius of Richland Center. Trout told me he always fished alone. He liked his solitude. He told me he planned to get out of the nursing home and get back on the trout stream as soon as he could. I looked at his frail, elderly form and wondered if he ever could. He must have seen the doubt in my face because he said, "Don't you worry about me. I'll get out of here one way or another."

I asked Trout how he got his nickname. As a young pup "Trout" was enamored with trout fishing. He spent every waking moment either trout fishing or talking about trout fishing. His grandfather gave him the nickname on a spring day when Trout caught a huge trout in a tiny stream near their home. *Trout's grandfather said: "Boy, you could catch a big trout in a mud puddle in the middle of Main Street."* The initial nickname was "Big Trout" but it morphed into Trout through the years.

I made many visits more to the nursing home to talk to Trout that winter. We always talked about trout fishing. I asked him if the four trout on his wall were the biggest trout he had ever landed. Trout's eyes squinted and the tone of his voice rose and a distinct sound of anger was there.

"There was this one SOB that got away at shore. It was a massive male brown. I played it for almost an hour and I had him next to shore and grabbed my net and tried to net him. That darn trout just straightened itself out in the net and made one more shake of its head and it got away.

"I can still remember the blasted thing mocking me as it slowly swam away, and I swear on my momma's grave that durn thing just turned right around just like it was lookin' right at me. Then it just swished its tail and it was gone." Trout turned and pointed to the huge net on the wall above his bed. He said: "I bought that net the next day. You'll never hear any "real" trout angler say "I wish I had a smaller net." I went right out that next day and bought three nets as big as Trout's.

Spring was approaching quickly and I was getting really fired up about opening day. I stopped to talk to Trout to pump him for some information on where he thought I should fish opening day. Trout looked at me and said he was quite puzzled. "You want me to tell you where to catch a big trout? Where is the fun in that? You need to earn your own trout. Get out there and catch a big one and report back to me on your outing on opening day. I don't want to hear about any little ones you caught."

Eight days flew by quickly and it was opening day. I caught a couple decent trout and lost one big one. I thought about what Trout had said throughout the winter. I fished all day and went to the nursing home at dark to tell Trout about the day. I walked directly to his room to talk to him. His bed was empty and all of his belongings were removed from his room . I was really freaked out. I went directly to the nurse's station. I was afraid to ask the charge nurse where Trout was. The charge nurse handed me a sealed envelope. It had "Spinner" written on the outside. I opened the envelope and read the shaky handwriting scrawled on the wrinkled paper inside.

"Dear Spinner,

By now you must have figured out I have moved on. I told you I'd get out of here one way or another. And at my age, I should be able to get what I want. Now I've been plannin' for a long time to just pack right up and get on outta here and do some real fishin'. And I am plumb sick and tired of sittin' on my old behind just talkin' about it, so I just went ahead and finally did it. Now don't you worry about me none. I'm doin' just fine. Just picture me on a perfect trout stream, and by golly, that's exactly where I am. Now don't go askin' the nurses about me, they'll just tell ya some cockamamie story that, well, just ain't true. And don't come lookin' for me none neither. I like my solitude and well, I just don't want to be found. Just consider me this...

Gone Fishin'
Trout Swenson"

I looked up at the nurse and she quickly looked away, tears in her eyes. The question rose up in my throat, stopped at the tip of my tongue, then faded away. I didn't need to ask. Trout had already explained it to me exactly the way he wanted me to understand it. There was nothing more to say. I turned and slowly walked out.

All of this happened the winter of 2001. I have not seen Trout on the streams and have not heard of him since our last lie swapping at the nursing home. I sometimes think of Trout when I am fishing these days. I smile when I remember Trout's eyes squinted and hearing the tone of his voice change and hearing about the big one that got away.

MORE MEN LIKE THEM

My dad was the ultimate sportsman. He tried every newfangled thing that he read about in the classic magazines, such as *Field & Stream* and *Outdoor Life*. He always read them at the local gas station with the rest of the hunting and fishing fans.

His interests were diverse. You could see him on the stream with a bamboo fly rod in the 1950s and 60s before bamboo became chic. Then you might be invited to the Harris Laboratory to help him make a recurve bow in the early 60s.

I always had a bird's eye view of all of the new projects. Being the only son, my dad thought I should watch and learn from each one of his ventures into the outdoors. He said even his failures were a learning experience.

I still remember the guys from the local gas station

coming to watch my father shoot his long bow in the back yard and watch him false cast in April with his bamboo fly rod. They all got their turns at casting and shooting these wonderful tools of the outdoors.

My dad would take out lots of the local young guys fishing and hunting. He tried to expose the young guys to the proper ways of being an outdoorsman. Proper meant cleaning up after yourself, and it also meant not harvesting any animal or fish you were not going to eat.

He would target the boys without a father or fathers that weren't outdoorsy. It was kind of a quest of his. He would say..."**If they respect the outdoors and can shoot a deer or clean a fish.....that's a good step to becoming a good man in adulthood.**" Lots of the lessons of the outdoors translate directly into regular day living. My dad was adamant about that.

I was too little in the beginning to go hunting so I pretty much went only fishing with him. We were always joined by one of the local young men. I was always a little jealous when Dad would head up north deer hunting and would have two or three of the local teenagers in tow to learn the ways of the outdoors.

I started going hunting with Dad at age eight. We went squirrel and pheasant hunting. I usually helped the dog flush birds or tree squirrels while my dad and his hunting friends shot them. It was really fun being out there. I would always listen to the lessons my dad gave to the local young bucks. I figured it would be my turn soon and I would have a leg up on this hunting thing because I listened very carefully to the lessons taught.

November 1967. My dad didn't get a deer locally so he

was going up north to his mother's home near Trego to deer hunt. He called all of the local kids to see if they wanted go. None could go. They either had filled their tags or had to stay close due to basketball practice. My dad left on his own the Wednesday before Thanksgiving to deer hunt in northern Wisconsin.

I know I'm jumping quite a ways ahead but it seemed like time flew after that. I was 16 years old and an accomplished angler already. My mother made sure she kept me in fishing poles and lures. Fishing can be done alone but young hunters need mentors to show them the ropes.

I yearned to go hunting. My mother seriously disliked hunting ever since 1967 when my father died while deer hunting. She forbid me to use any of my father's guns and sold off the majority of them. My mother told me I could use the one gun she saved for me when I was an adult and not before then.

It was opening day of squirrel season. I went to the local gas station and saw all the guys talking about how good the squirrel hunting was. One of the guys that my dad had taken in the past was there. He asked how my opener hunt had gone. I told him about my mother's rule about hunting. He was really taken aback. He couldn't believe that Lenny Harris' son was not allowed to go hunting.

It was Sunday morning about noon. There was knock on the door. I answered it. It was Jim Chellevold, the guy from the gas station from the day before. He wanted to talk to my mom. He reminded my mother about how Dad had taken him hunting as a teenager and how he loved the outdoors because of my dad. He asked if he could take me squirrel hunting. My mother hemmed and hawed for a while but she finally broke down and let him take me.

Jim took me to the local gas station and he bought me my small game license and a box of 410 shells. We went back to my house and we inspected the pump 410 that had not been used in six years, ever since my dad died. Jim gave me a quick refresher on hunting safety in front of my mother to satisfy her and off we went squirrel hunting.

We came home three hours later and cleaned our squirrels in the back yard. Those three hours of squirrel hunting with Jim were beyond description. Jim told tall tales of when my dad had taken him hunting and fishing. He told me about Dad calling and wanting to take him along in 1967. Jim had already filled his tag.

My mother was softened by the kindheartedness of Jim and allowed me to go hunting then. I went hunting a few more times with Jim and he taught me all of the things I missed from not having my dad teach me.

My mother's oldest brother Sig took me under his wing and helped me a lot with hunting. Uncle Sig and his son Sig Jr. were instrumental in me becoming the man I am today. They showed me the ways of the woods and safety with a gun. Uncle Sig is hunting deer in heaven with my Dad now but Sig Jr. is still around. He still has that burning desire to hunt. He has passed it on to his son Roman and my other cousin Wade.

I am saying thank you in this story to all the men from Reber's Gas Station that helped me become the man I am today. With a **special thank you to my Uncle Sig and Cousin Sig**. I wish there were more men like Jim/Judd/John/Ernie/Vic/Geno/Cheesy/Rod/Pat in the world.

Thanks
Are you one of those MEN?

THE STREAM OF TIME

I was startled awake by the alarm clock. I couldn't figure out why the blasted thing was squawking in my ear at 3:00 a.m., so I sat up and reached across the bed to turn the infernal thing off. As I lay down to go back to sleep my bride of forty-one years elbowed me and said: "Get out of bed, Peter, you old fool." I responded: "I am retired now, I thought we threw that alarm clock away!" to which she replied: "Len is expecting you at four." It then dawned upon me "I am going trout fishing today!" I sprang from my bed.

Sprang is a relative word. As sprang as any 62 year-old, recently retired school teacher can sprang, today was the day. I was going to re-introduce myself to my childhood passion—trout fishing. I quietly left the bedroom and started a pot of coffee. As the coffee brewed, all the memories of my childhood fishing rushed over me. The day I was bitten by the trout fishing bug was crystal clear in my mind . It seemed just like yesterday. I have played that memory over and over again in my head many times. It usually happens when the first cold snap hits in late September.

Dad rolled me out of bed at the crack of dawn. Uncle Don is already in the car, waiting. The gear is packed and all that's left is to get me dressed and into the car. Dad hurries me and tells me that we need to be on the water before it gets too sunny. Dad turns the old Buick westward. We are on our way.

Dad and Uncle Don are giddy with anticipation, and as they reminisce about old outings they took together when they were young Dad tells me about the first time he went fishing with his father. I had heard that story many times and smiled as he told it again. The fish he'd caught had grown since the last time I'd heard it!

The road gets long and I nod off. All of a sudden Dad and Uncle Don are almost shouting: "Here's the bridge", Uncle Don exclaims. He bolts from the Buick, gets down on all fours and crawls up to the bridge's edge. He peers over the bridge, then crawls back and comes running to the car. Uncle Don is really fired up. He says: "Young man, there are a couple nice browns under that bridge with your name written on them!"

My Dad places me downstream from the bridge. Uncle Don is in the sneak position again. He crawls to the edge of the bridge to aid me in placing my cast properly. Dad directs my cast with the aid of Uncle Don. It seems just like yesterday. The beautiful brown trout takes my offering on the first cast. My dad and uncle are cheering me. The battle seems infinite. I land a smallish brown. My dad and uncle make me feel like that trout was the biggest and most beautiful trout they had ever seen. A farmer in a truck drove by at the same time and gave me a thumb up as he drove across the bridge.

Man, did I ever get sidetracked.

I had to get moving and meet up with Len. The time is just screaming by, just like all those years of teaching had. I had never gotten a chance to go back to that bridge. Teaching and family had washed away any chance of getting back there.

I met up with Len and we got into his truck for the trip to the bridge. I did not remember the exact area of the bridge as I was six years old the last time there and I had slept almost all the way there; I just knew a general area of the bridge. As Len drove along I tried to describe what the bridge looked like.

I told Len the story about my first outing with Dad and Uncle Don. I described the bridge to a "t." The way my uncle had hung off the bridge on his belly to direct my first cast. We searched and searched the area. We could not find the bridge. We stopped and looked at the map to see if there was a place we were missing. I was so sad. I could not find that bridge... it had disappeared. I could not talk with my dad or uncle. They both had been taken by the stream of time to where all good anglers go. We finally gave up on the bridge and turned around and decided to hit some close water.

Len slowed the truck and said: "Peter, is that it out in the field?" I said: "No, it can't be. It isn't the way I remember it. It was on the main road and it didn't look like that." Len told me that the county had straightened the road about 35 years ago and made a new bridge. That bridge out in the field had to be it.

Len could see my disappointment. I got out of the truck and strung up my rod. I asked Len if I could fish the stretch alone. I wanted to try to re-capture some of the magic of my ancient memories. Everything looked different. I thought to myself that this couldn't be the bridge. I carefully approached the bridge hole... I placed my first cast directly in the feed lane. A brown trout came up and took my presentation. I knelt down to net the brown... the memories rushed back... the bridge ruins jolted my memory.

Don't let The Stream of Time wash you away before you have found *YOUR* bridge.

About the Author: Len Harris was born in Milwaukee, Wisconsin in June 1957, one of six children of Jane and Len Harris Sr. His mother and father decided the big city was no place to raise a growing family, so they moved to Gays Mills, Wisconsin. There, life was simple for Len Jr. until he was ten. Then things drastically changed with the death of his father.

Len followed in his father's footsteps and continued hunting and fishing in the hills and valleys of southwestern Wisconsin. His father had given him the love of the outdoors and his mother cultivated that love. The outdoors taught him many life lessons that he uses to this day.

Len married Barb Jurgensen from that same small town where he grew up. They have one beautiful daughter named Anna. The family resides only 32 miles from their hometown. Len has shared his love of the outdoors with his family. He also has shared those memories in written form in numerous publications.

Len is a staff writer and photographer for Midwest Outdoors. He also does freelance work and has appeared in American Angler and Field & Stream. There are numerous other magazines and newspapers that Len writes for. His love for trout fishing has been shared on numerous Midwestern television shows. He also does quite a few presentations at local schools to spread his love for the outdoors to the youth of the area. Len recently started speaking at nursing homes. He says:, "They can't go to the streams anymore so I bring the streams to them."

Made in the USA
Charleston, SC
05 February 2013